ABOLISHING NUCLEAR WEAPONS

GEORGE PERKOVICH AND JAMES M. ACTON

ADELPHI PAPER 396

The International Institute for Strategic Studies

Arundel House | 13–15 Arundel Street | Temple Place | London | WC2R 3DX | UK

ADELPHI PAPER 396

First published August 2008 by **Routledge**
4 Park Square, Milton Park, Abingdon, Oxon, OX14 4RN

for **The International Institute for Strategic Studies**
Arundel House, 13–15 Arundel Street, Temple Place, London, WC2R 3DX, UK
www.iiss.org

Simultaneously published in the USA and Canada by **Routledge**
270 Madison Ave., New York, NY 10016

Routledge is an imprint of Taylor & Francis, an Informa Business

© 2008 The International Institute for Strategic Studies

DIRECTOR-GENERAL AND CHIEF EXECUTIVE John Chipman
EDITOR Tim Huxley
MANAGER FOR EDITORIAL SERVICES Ayse Abdullah
ASSISTANT EDITOR Katharine Fletcher
PRODUCTION John Buck
COVER IMAGE PA

Printed and bound in Great Britain by Bell & Bain Ltd, Thornliebank, Glasgow

British Library Cataloguing in Publication Data
A catalogue record for this book is available from the British Library

Library of Congress Cataloging in Publication Data
A catalogue record for this book is available from the Library of Congress

ISBN 978-0-415-46583-0
ISSN 0567-932X

Contents

GLOSSARY

CTBT	Comprehensive Test Ban Treaty
CWC	Chemical Weapons Convention
FMCT	Fissile Material Cut-Off Treaty
HEU	Highly enriched uranium
IAEA	International Atomic Energy Agency
INF	Intermediate Nuclear Forces (Treaty)
LEU	Low-enriched uranium
MOX	Mixed-oxide fuel
NPT	Nuclear Non-Proliferation Treaty
P5	The five permanent members of the United Nations Security Council
START	Strategic Arms Reduction Treaty

INTRODUCTION

This paper aims to encourage a conversation about the abolition of nuclear weapons. How might the security conditions which would permit nuclear weapons to be safely prohibited be created, and how might measures to implement such a prohibition be verified and enforced?[1]

Over the past couple of years, there has been a growing awareness of the need to take nuclear disarmament seriously. In January 2007, and again in January 2008, the *Wall Street Journal* published articles by US statesmen George Shultz, William Perry, Henry Kissinger and Sam Nunn calling for invigorated movement towards the goal of a world free of nuclear weapons and urging other former high-level officials around the world to endorse this goal.[2] In recent months, four former defence and foreign ministers of the United Kingdom representing each of the country's leading political parties have joined their call,[3] which has also been echoed by governments. Most prominently, a number of senior UK cabinet ministers, including the prime minister, Gordon Brown, have proposed concrete steps that states could take jointly to help create the conditions necessary for the abolition of nuclear weapons,[4] as has Indian Prime Minister Manmohan Singh.[5]

What appears to have motivated much of this interest is the belief that it will be impossible to curtail nuclear-weapons proliferation without serious progress towards nuclear disarmament. In the absence of sufficient action on disarmament by the nuclear-weapons states, leaders of many non-nuclear-weapons states are increasingly resistant to efforts to strengthen the International Atomic Energy Agency (IAEA) system of nuclear safeguards that is designed to ensure that civilian nuclear facilities are not used for military purposes. They also insist that they will not accept any new discriminatory constraints on their access to nuclear technology. Resistance to stronger non-proliferation measures is especially worrying given the expectation of a significant global expansion in nuclear-energy production. Ultimately, if it is to be sustainable and acceptable to the majority of states, any new nuclear order must be equitable and not perpetuate the disparity between the states that possess nuclear weapons and those that do not.

What is needed now is for a conversation about disarmament to take place between officials and experts from non-nuclear-weapons states and those from nuclear-weapons states. There has not been such a conversation for a long time. Diplomats gather every five years at conferences to review the Nuclear Non-Proliferation Treaty (NPT), but they do not seriously discuss the substantive conditions necessary to achieve the verifiable and enforceable elimination of all nuclear arsenals. These conferences, operating by consensus rules, have often been unproductive. The sixty-five-member Conference on Disarmament, established in 1979 as a result of a UN General Assembly special session on disarmament to serve a multilateral negotiating forum, is currently moribund. Representatives of nuclear-weapons states pay lip service to the principle of nuclear disarmament, but none of these states has an employee, let alone an inter-agency group, tasked full time with figuring out what would be required to verifiably decommission all its nuclear weapons. Non-nuclear-weapons states have not really engaged with the challenge either, in spite of their disarmament rhetoric. They have tended to view disarmament as something that the nuclear-weapons states should undertake and report back on when it is accomplished.

The need for non-nuclear-weapons states to join a debate over the details of nuclear disarmament is great. The global diffusion of the technology and know-how to produce fissile materials threatens to overwhelm the existing regime to prevent the 'diversion of nuclear energy from peaceful uses to nuclear weapons'.[6] Fear of nuclear proliferation is motivating some nuclear-weapons states to take nuclear disarmament more seriously,[7] but neither non-proliferation nor the abolition of nuclear weapons can be achieved without the active cooperation of non-nuclear-weapons states. Nuclear abolition would require much more than the dismantling of all nuclear weapons in the nine states that now possess them. To make abolition feasible and to enable the detection of rearmament, all states that possess nuclear reactors, uranium-enrichment plants, plutonium-reprocessing facilities, uranium reserves or even transshipment ports would have to accept more intrusive control measures and inspection procedures than they do today. To build confidence that an agreement to prohibit nuclear weapons would be enforced, all states would need to demonstrate a willingness to enforce international rules with greater alacrity and robustness than has been historically normal.

Discussions of this paper's early drafts suggested that experts in non-nuclear-weapons states felt at times insufficiently informed on technical details and/or that these issues were too low among their national priorities for them to be able to fruitfully debate them with their counterparts in nuclear-weapons states. Some nuclear-weapons-state officials appear happy to reinforce such feelings. What ensues, then, is (often heated) debate between factions within states that possess nuclear weapons over what types of inspection protocol would be necessary to verify nuclear disarmament, or whether the permanent members of the UN Security Council would retain veto rights in a world without nuclear weapons. Frequently these debates are limited to the US, the UK and, to a lesser extent, India, as nuclear policy is not a major subject for discussion in France (where there is not much public interest in the subject), and information is tightly controlled in Russia, China, Israel, Pakistan and North Korea. There is little substantive give-and-take on disarmament issues between informed citizens and officials from nuclear-weapons states and many non-nuclear-weapons states, whether the topic is, for instance, how to guarantee the supply of nuclear fuel to actors that forgo indigenous uranium enrichment, or how to deter cheating in a nuclear-weapons-free world.

Theoretically, the eight states that have acquired nuclear weapons without violating international treaties (henceforth referred to as the 'nuclear-armed states' to distinguish them from the five states among them that are recognised by the NPT) could create a forum for negotiating an agreement to prohibit nuclear weapons. In today's world, however, states are more likely to proceed in an ad hoc, incremental manner. Aside from the Conference on Disarmament, there is currently no diplomatic structure pertaining to nuclear affairs that includes the five NPT-recognised nuclear-weapons states plus India, Pakistan and Israel. The latter three states are not party to the NPT, nor are they permanent members of the UN Security Council. While there is no legal reason why the nuclear-armed states could not create an informal process to pursue nuclear disarmament, they are too ambivalent about the objective to muster the collective energy and resources to do so. Even if motivations were stronger, states would still be deterred by the expectation that some non-nuclear-weapons states would object to such a process on the grounds that it would grant unacceptable status to the three non-parties to the NPT.

We will suggest at the conclusion of this paper that internationally respected think tanks – including some affiliated with governments – could initiate a high-level unofficial panel in which experts and officials from non-nuclear-weapons states could join with those from nuclear-armed states to explore how the myriad challenges of verifiably and securely eliminating nuclear arsenals might be addressed. Such unofficial explorations could prepare the ground for official engagement with these issues when political conditions allow. Ideally, governments would augment these explorations by encouraging additional relevant nuclear-weapons experts, laboratory officials and military strategists to participate.

The debate that this paper seeks to facilitate is about how complete nuclear disarmament could be achieved safely and securely, not whether it should be tried. Some commentators on earlier drafts charged us with minimising the difficulties of nuclear abolition. They suggested that our belief in the desirability of abolition blinded us to its infeasibility. Others have said that we have identified too many obstacles, and that the paper should not be published in case it disappoints those who desire total nuclear disarmament, turning them further against initiatives to prevent proliferation, which they may see as merely advantaging the nuclear-armed states. To be clear, we believe that nuclear-weapons states have political and moral obligations to seek to eliminate all nuclear arsenals. These obligations stem from Article VI of the NPT, which specifies that parties should pursue negotiations leading to complete nuclear disarmament,[8] the 1995 negotiations over indefinite extension of the treaty, and the basic principle that a nuclear order cannot be maintained and strengthened over time on the basis of inequity. Double standards on matters as materially and psychologically important as nuclear weapons will produce instability and non-compliance, creating enforcement crises that increase the risk of conflict and nuclear anarchy.[9] Lawyers, diplomats and military commanders may debate the relevance and precise meaning of Article VI of the NPT. But it is clear that states would not have agreed to extend the treaty indefinitely, as they did in 1995, if the nuclear-weapons states had tried to claim that they were not obliged to pursue nuclear disarmament. In any case, the problem of states resisting strengthened non-proliferation rules because they say they are frustrated by the nuclear-weapons states' refusal to uphold their side of the NPT bargain must be addressed. More generally, so long as large ready-to-launch nuclear arsenals exist (and especially if more states acquire nuclear weapons), the risk that these weapons will one day be detonated is not negligible. For these reasons, we do not argue why disarmament is desirable, except briefly in the conclusions.

None of this, of course, makes nuclear-weapons abolition feasible. Indeed, it is easy to say why it is not. Conversely, it is difficult to show how conditions could be created that would encourage states to make a nuclear-weapons prohibition verifiable and enforceable. This is the challenge that motivates us here. Our specific aims are twofold: first, to identify and explore the challenges to the complete abolition of nuclear weapons, and second, to discuss what states can start doing today to circumvent them. We do not claim to exhaust the range of issues that must be resolved, or to have optimally framed the subjects we do address. If there are places where we appear defeated by obstacles that could be dismissed or better navigated, we welcome other people's responses.

We do want to dispatch one objection at the outset. It is sometimes said that nuclear weapons 'cannot be disinvented'. We recognise this, but believe that the point is made to deflect careful thinking rather than encourage it. No human creation can be disinvented. Civilization has nevertheless prohibited and dismantled artefacts deemed too dangerous, damaging or morally objectionable to continue living with. Mass-scale gas chambers such as those used by Nazi Germany have not been disinvented, but they are not tolerated. The CFCs (chlorofluorocarbons) that created a hole in the ozone layer cannot be disinvented, but they have been prohibited with great benefit and other means have been found to perform their functions. The issue is rather whether means could exist to verify that a rejected technology – nuclear weapons in this theoretical case – had been dismantled everywhere, and to minimise the risk of cheating. Ultimately, the challenges of verification and enforcement could be so daunting that states would choose not to prohibit and dismantle all nuclear weapons, but the question of 'disinvention' should not deter us from this exploration.

Some readers may conclude that the difficulties and costs we identify of moving from the last few weapons to zero are so great that we should have focused more on the benefits and relative ease of earlier steps. One commentator on an early draft spoke for several when he said, 'Why don't you highlight the value of reducing nuclear arsenals to a few tens of nuclear weapons, and posturing them for no-first-use, and treating them as anathema, hidden-in-the-basement weapons of last resort? That world would be much less threatening than today's, and we shouldn't let the difficulties of getting to perfect zero keep us from it.'

We agree absolutely that the challenges of getting to zero do not and should not preclude many steps being taken in that direction. Mindful of this admonition, therefore, we address in the first chapter steps that nuclear-armed states could take in cooperation with others towards a world in which tackling the more difficult task of prohibiting nuclear weapons could be envisaged.

The remainder of the paper focuses on the more distant prospect of actually prohibiting nuclear weapons. It is tempting to avoid exploring some of the crucial difficulties involved in going to zero by saying, 'problems of enforcement and international politics would naturally be worked out on the way towards zero, or else states would not agree ultimately to create a nuclear-weapon-free world'. We believe this is inadequate. States will not begin to make the changes necessary for abolishing nuclear weapons if there is not a shared sense that the goal is realistic. And states cannot demonstrate their real commitment to this goal if they do not understand and accept the challenge of trying to implement the changes that must be made along the way.

Chapter 2 examines some of the greatest verification challenges of going from low numbers of nuclear weapons to zero. Although this chapter does discuss some essentially political questions, such as how good verification would need to be for states to feel enough confidence to eliminate their arsenals, it is largely technical. This cannot be avoided; nuclear abolition is an interdisciplinary problem that requires politicians, diplomats and non-governmental experts to engage with technical issues.

The third chapter explores the implications of nuclear-weapons abolition for the management of the forecast spread of nuclear energy to new markets. The risk of civilian-use fissile materials or expertise being diverted to make nuclear weapons is tolerated today in large part because major powers (and others) retain nuclear weapons that are felt to deter both proliferation and nuclear aggression from states cheating on their non-proliferation obligations. But tolerance of the risks associated with nuclear power would be much lower if all nuclear arsenals were eliminated. On the other hand, the equity of a world in which all states forswore nuclear weapons, and worked actively towards their elimination, could facilitate the establishment and enforcement of more robust rules to ensure that the growing number of states seeking nuclear-energy capabilities used them exclusively for peaceful purposes.

Chapter 4 imagines that the political and security conditions had been created to motivate negotiations on prohibiting nuclear weapons worldwide, and explores key practical questions that would need to be resolved for states to have confidence that a prohibition would be enforced effectively. This discussion is necessarily speculative, and is intended to stimulate further international analysis and debate, rather than resolve the complex issues involved.

Chapter 5 examines the issue of hedging. Were all nuclear arsenals to be dismantled, the states that had possessed them would still retain know-how and probably some infrastructure that would enable them to reconstitute at least a small number of nuclear weapons rather quickly. This latency might represent an inescapable problem, or a desirable means of deterring or retaliating against cheating, or indeed both. In this chapter we explore some of the pros and cons of 'virtual' arsenals and international control of a minimal deterrent, and examine approaches to the management of nuclear-weapons know-how.

The conclusions come full circle by responding to the question, 'why bother with nuclear abolition?'. After citing five global security interests that would be served by fully fledged efforts to create a nuclear-weapons-free world, we suggest that the only way to resolve the 'who goes first?' problem among nuclear-weapons and non-nuclear-weapons states is to move on both the disarmament and non-proliferation fronts simultaneously. We recognise that governments could be informed and inspired to pursue reciprocating steps if unofficial advance work were done by international experts, a process to which this paper seeks to modestly contribute. The paper ends with an appendix summarising key questions and suggestions that it has outlined.

Establishing Political Conditions to Enhance the Feasibility of Abolishing Nuclear Weapons

Where are we now?

Some observers posit that none of today's nuclear-armed states would fall prey to major aggression if they all eliminated their nuclear arsenals. A proportion go further and argue that if all nuclear-armed states made a credible agreement to eliminate their arsenals, the rest of the world would pitch in by agreeing to support a much more robust collective security system that would act against any actor that newly sought to threaten others. In this sense, nuclear abolition could help cause a reduction in threats and a strengthening of security.

Others would say that this was nonsense. States possess nuclear weapons because they fear they might face threats of massive destruction. If they all got rid of nuclear weapons, major warfare might not break out immediately, but the chances of such conflict coming about would rise dramatically. The sense of threat felt by states can be reduced only over time, through former adversaries demonstrating that they recognise they have no interest in warring against each other – that doing so would cause the instigator more harm than good. Nuclear deterrence is one way to build cautious, war-avoiding interests. If it is to be traded away, some other reliable means must substitute for it.

Whatever the merits of these arguments, reality has put the states that possess nuclear weapons in the driver's seat, albeit while travelling a road that may lead over a cliff. They cannot be forced to eliminate these weapons. They will choose to do so only if they judge that they will not become more endangered as a result. They will insist that prohibition of nuclear weapons does not 'make the world safe' for conventional war among major powers.

This is not a fair demand. It is motivated by the assumption that nuclear weapons would never fail to deter major conventional war, and it neglects the consequences if deterrence fails and nuclear weapons are detonated. Demanding that a nuclear-weapons-free world provide as much deterrence as is now ascribed to the current nuclear order, but with less risk, underestimates the benefits of living without the threat of destruction that even modest-sized nuclear arsenals project. Nevertheless, as a political and psychological matter, people contemplating losing things they already have tend to place higher value on them than do people who have never possessed them. Then-UK Prime Minister Tony Blair reflected this psychology in December 2006, when he announced his government's decision to build a replacement for the UK Navy's *Vanguard*-class nuclear submarines: 'There are perfectly respectable arguments against the judgement we have made', Blair told Parliament:

> It's just that, in the final analysis, the risk of giving up something that has been one of the mainstays of our security since the war, and, moreover, doing so when the one certain thing about our world today is its uncertainty, is not a risk I feel we can responsibly take.[1]

This loss aversion among decision-makers – which should also be assumed to be influenced by concern about the loss aversion of the voting public – is a political reality that efforts to prohibit nuclear weapons will need to confront.

Perhaps the best that can be practically expected of the nuclear-armed states is that they agree to work incrementally, in reciprocating steps, towards nuclear disarmament. These states make it clear that they will not eliminate their nuclear arsenals unilaterally; indeed, many officials and observers in nuclear-armed states mistakenly fear that this is what disarmament advocates demand of them. The new commander of US strategic forces, General Kevin Chilton, recently illustrated this misunderstanding when he was asked at a US Senate hearing what he thought of Shultz et al's calls for states to pursue nuclear disarmament: 'As a father … I would … love to envision a world someday free of nuclear weapons; but I also envision … a world that is free for my children and grandchildren to grow up in', Chilton said. 'I'm not for unilateral disarmament … Unilateral disarmament will not preserve that [freedom] in a world where other countries possess nuclear weapons, particularly in quantities enough that could destroy our way of life if they should decide to use them against us.'[2] But neither the NPT nor most calls for a nuclear-weapons-free world envisage that the US, Russia, China and other nuclear-armed states would eliminate all their nuclear weapons unilaterally; rather, the objective is for all states to create the conditions that would enable the mutual, verifiable and enforceable elimination of all nuclear arsenals. Chilton's formulation was in fact more promising for nuclear disarmament than is commonly thought, as he conditioned his advocacy for retaining US nuclear weapons only on the existence of nuclear weapons elsewhere in quantities sufficient to 'destroy' the US 'way of life'. Unlike officials in other nuclear-armed states, for example France and Russia, he did not suggest that the US needed to keep nuclear weapons to deal with non-nuclear threats.

Global nuclear disarmament is too far beyond the horizon for leaders of the US, Russia, China, France, the UK, Israel, India and Pakistan to form a consensus now on how and when it would be achieved. There are too many actors, too many unforeseeable possible technological innovations, and too many political and security-related events that could intervene for today's possessors of nuclear weapons to be able to codify in the near future all the political steps and the verification and enforcement procedures that would be required to prohibit nuclear weapons. Individuals and think tanks can be more venturesome, and offer policies and procedures for verifying and enforcing a global prohibition on nuclear weapons, as we do in this paper. However, current leaders can and should be expected to identify practical, concrete steps they can take in the near term to advance towards a horizon from which their successors could visualise achieving a prohibition on nuclear weapons. Moreover, as we argue in subsequent chapters, there is much that states can do today, short of formal negotiations, to begin the process of solving the problems which would threaten to become major obstacles as numbers approached zero.

William Walker urges that nuclear abolition be approached as a 'co-evolutionary' process of reciprocal step-by-step progress, in which non-proliferation and arms-reduction measures emerge from changed political and security environments and vice versa.[3] Different sets of states will need to take different steps, but all must move gradually in the same direction. Ultimately, in order for a secure, verifiable prohibition to be established, many bodies will need to walk in step; but in the early years of the process, different pairs or small groups of states would focus on each other. Some will move faster and more smoothly than others to ameliorate political and security tensions and implement nuclear reductions and controls. Deadlines could speed the process, but the political will to establish them has not yet been generated in any of the nuclear-armed states, with the exception of India.[4] Moreover, as emphasised throughout this paper, for a prohibition to be feasible, non-nuclear-weapons states too would need to change their policies and practices. Their willingness to negotiate and implement the steps that would be needed to make the world safe for disarmament should not be taken for granted.

To examine current and possible future conditions in more detail, we begin at the 'top', with the two states which today have nuclear arsenals that clearly exceed their minimal security requirements, the US and Russia. We then briefly discuss the current disposition of France and the UK, before turning to China. In many ways, China is pivotal. Its political and security concerns are based substantially on its assessments of US and Russian strategic intentions and capabilities (which are affected by China in turn), while China's intentions and capabilities affect the calculations of India and, therefore, Pakistan. (China also affects Japan and South Korea, which have capabilities and interests that could lead them to produce nuclear weapons quickly, and who currently shelter under the US nuclear 'umbrella'). After discussing Chinese considerations, we turn to the regional political and security dynamics that most immediately concern India, Pakistan and Israel. We examine too the unresolved sovereignty issues in Northeast Asia, South Asia and the Middle East that have a major bearing on the retention and possible proliferation of nuclear weapons. The US also affects the proliferation potential of each of these regions, as do China, Russia, the UK and France to varying degrees.

In each of these contexts, conventional military dynamics cannot be ignored. In addition to exploring these dynamics, we also address the challenge of maintaining extended deterrence in the years leading up to disarmament. We consider too the role of ballistic-missile defence and concerns about the threat of nuclear terrorism, before concluding this chapter with near-term steps that states could take to demonstrate resolve to improve the feasibility of prohibiting nuclear weapons.

US and Russian early steps
The US currently possesses an estimated 5,400 operational nuclear warheads, of which 1,260 are held in reserve in an inactive stockpile. An additional 5,000 are awaiting dismantlement. There are approximately 5,200 nuclear warheads in Russia's operational stockpile, and a further 8,800 in reserve or awaiting dismantlement.[5] Thousands of US and Russian

weapons are deployed so that they could be launched within minutes. Neither state forswears first use of nuclear weapons; both leave open the possibility of using nuclear weapons pre-emptively or in response to non-nuclear threats, and maintain the capability to do so. Many commentators have noted that these quick-use forces could exacerbate instability in crises, and are vulnerable to inadvertent use as a result of false warnings or system malfunction. Leaders of both countries insist that they do not foresee threats from each other that would warrant the mutual destructiveness of nuclear exchanges, but they have not brought their arsenals into quantitative or operational alignment with their political and security relationship.

This paper need not make the case for the well-known steps that the US and Russia could and should take now to reduce unnecessary dangers. Shultz, Perry, Kissinger and Nunn in their 2007 and 2008 *Wall Street Journal* articles urged Moscow and Washington to extend the verification provisions of their Strategic Arms Reduction Treaty (START I) and to undertake further rounds of nuclear-force reductions. They called for steps to be taken towards increasing the warning and decision times for the launch of all nuclear-armed ballistic missiles, and the discarding of any operational plans for massive attacks. They also asked the US to adopt a process for bringing the Comprehensive Test Ban Treaty (CTBT) into effect.[6] The Luxembourg Forum, a private initiative sponsored by a Russian foundation and run by independent Russian experts with governmental experience, endorsed the recommendations made by Shultz et al. in their January 2007 article, as well as additional steps, at a May 2007 conference of 57 leading international arms-control and disarmament experts.[7]

It is entirely fair to say that if the new leaders of the two states do not take initiatives to further reduce the size, roles and political–strategic prominence of their nuclear arsenals, the overall project of nuclear disarmament cannot proceed. This may suit Russian leaders: a Russian analyst who commented on early drafts of this paper remarked that it was 'not a good career move to talk about nuclear disarmament in Russia today'. Clearly, the attitudes and policies of the new US administration in 2009 will affect Russia's interests and political will regarding disarmament. Yet the rest of the international community should recognise that Russia's positions are not merely reactive to the US, and that Russia in its own right can facilitate or retard the evolution of a more secure global nuclear order. Those officials who want nuclear disarmament to progress will need to engage their Russian counterparts directly on this agenda.

France

France has signed and ratified the CTBT, and shut down and dismantled its facilities for the production of fissile materials for explosive purposes. It has also dismantled its nuclear-testing facility. In March 2008, President Sarkozy announced that France was further reducing its nuclear arsenal so that it would be left with 'fewer than 300 nuclear warheads'.[8]

While this record is laudable, in private conversations, French officials do not hide their distaste for the idea of totally eliminating nuclear arsenals. In the run-up to the 2005 NPT Review Conference, France joined the US Bush administration in refusing to reaffirm the 'unequivocal undertaking ... to accomplish the total elimination of their nuclear arsenals' that the nuclear-weapons states had made at the 2000 conference.[9] French officials have exerted pressure on other countries to refrain from advocating visions of a world without nuclear weapons.[10] Most problematically, France's rationale for wielding nuclear weapons is open-ended and not based on the existence of nuclear threats against France. As Sarkozy has put it, 'our nuclear deterrence protects us from any aggression against our vital interests emanating from a state – wherever it may come from and whatever form it may take'.[11] By not tying its possession of nuclear weapons to the possession of them by others, France gives the impression that it seeks to keep nuclear weapons regardless of what others do. France's rationale is so broad that any aspiring proliferator could say that it wanted nuclear weapons for the same reasons. The only answer to this position would be that the aspiring proliferator had signed a treaty committing it to not acquiring nuclear weapons. But France's aversion to the idea of eliminating all nuclear arsenals undermines the core bargain of the NPT, which makes the treaty a weaker basis for insisting that others not acquire these weapons. Nevertheless, the US and Russia have much work to do to bring their nuclear forces and infrastructure down to a level where France (or the UK) could be expected to take further major disarmament initiatives.

In sum, while France has taken exemplary steps to reduce its nuclear arsenal, and has been a creative leader in trying to strengthen the nuclear non-proliferation regime, it does not place itself in the vanguard of efforts to establish the feasibility of abolishing nuclear weapons.

The United Kingdom

The United Kingdom has announced it will reduce its stockpile of operational nuclear warheads to 'no more than 160'.[12] Unlike all other nuclear-armed states, the UK bases its nuclear deterrent only at sea, and has no land- or air-based nuclear weapons. The UK has ratified the CTBT and halted production of fissile materials for weapons purposes.

Though official discussions of the country's nuclear deterrent have tended to speak of deterring major nuclear threats, the UK has not excluded nuclear deterrence of other threats, such as from biological or chemical weapons, and has declined to give promises of no first use. However, UK officials have juxtaposed their current unwillingness to abandon nuclear weapons unilaterally with allusions to a 'global move' towards complete nuclear disarmament that would present the UK with a different decision-making calculus. The UK has in many ways taken the lead among recognised nuclear-weapons states in embracing the objective of a nuclear-weapons-free world. Unlike French officials, for example, UK leaders have made explicit statements in favour of multilateral nuclear disarmament. In February 2008, Defence Secretary Des Browne volunteered that:

> The international community needs a transparent, sustainable and credible plan for multilateral nuclear disarmament … The UK has a vision of a world free of nuclear weapons and, in partnership with everyone who shares that ambition, we intend to make further progress towards this vision in the coming years.[13]

China

China has exhibited exceptional restraint in the development of its nuclear weapons and the political–military prominence it gives to them. Its nuclear weapons are intended to provide deterrence through retaliation within days, rather than minutes or hours, of undergoing an attack.[14] It deploys approximately 130 nuclear warheads for delivery by land-based missiles, sea-based missiles and aircraft. Combined with additional warheads believed to be in storage, this makes for a total stockpile of fewer than 200.[15] China continues to insist that it will not use nuclear weapons first, and it has a bilateral agreement with Russia to this effect. The country is, however, modernising and increasing the number of its nuclear delivery systems and possibly warheads, with a clear intention of reducing its vulnerability to US or Russian attack. The pace and extent of this modernisation and expansion has consistently lagged behind US intelligence estimates, although this could change.[16] In the absence of assurances from Russia and – especially – the US about the future quantity and quality of their nuclear forces, and their plans for ballistic missile defences, China has not indicated what, if any, limits it envisages for its future nuclear arsenal.

Chinese officials insist that they favour nuclear disarmament and would be prepared to join an arms-reduction process once states with larger nuclear arsenals, particularly the US and Russia, had significantly reduced these arsenals. However, private discussions with strategic analysts affiliated with the People's Liberation Army and the Chinese nuclear-weapons establishment indicate that there are grave doubts in China that the US and Russia could pursue nuclear disarmament in ways that would alleviate China's insecurities to the point where it would feel secure without a small survivable nuclear armoury (i.e., one that could survive an adversary's first strike and deliver a retaliatory attack). We discuss below several key strategic issues related to offensive nuclear forces, ballistic-missile defences and non-nuclear strike capabilities that China would want to have addressed before it would consider joining a nuclear-arms-reduction process. Still, Chinese authorities and analysts would be making a contribution to global security if they began internal deliberations now to specify what level of US and Russian reductions would be sufficient to induce China to join an arms-reduction process. This would give the international community a better sense of how and when a global move towards nuclear disarmament could be envisaged.

India

India is estimated to possess between 50 and 60 nuclear warheads.[17] It could deliver these weapons with aircraft or land-based missiles, and is developing a seaborne capability, including plans for nuclear-powered submarines that could deploy ballistic missiles. India continues to modernise and expand its nuclear-weapons-production infrastructure, its fissile-material and weapons stockpiles, and its delivery systems. Yet India does not evince an arms-race mentality. Its leadership generally shows restraint, and gives the sense that nuclear weapons are regrettable political weapons of last resort, not militarily useful instruments. India does not deploy nuclear weapons on alert; it maintains its nuclear warheads apart from delivery systems. It insists that it would never use nuclear weapons first, though it qualifies this commitment in the case of responses to chemical- or biological-weapons attack.

Most importantly for the theme of this paper, India has not abandoned its long tradition of advocating complete nuclear disarmament. It insists that the objective be pursued globally and without discrimination. Only in this way, it believes, would Indian security interests be served and its political concerns put to rest. In particular, Pakistan and China would have to shed their nuclear weapons, and India would need to have confidence in its conventional military balance in relation to both. The disarmament of all other current nuclear-armed states, particularly the US and the UK, would symbolise the equity India has sought in international politics since independence. India could, however, make demands that would complicate a disarmament process, some of which are discussed further in Chapter 4. The former Indian foreign secretary, Shyam Saran, now the prime minister's nuclear envoy, has criticised the approach of Shultz et al. by suggesting that their real priority might be to tighten a discriminatory technology-denial regime and coerce 'rogue' states.[18] India might test the other nuclear-armed states' seriousness by proposing timebound steps toward nuclear disarmament, including no-first-use commitments. Most, if not all, other nuclear-armed states are highly resistant to the idea of committing to the elimination of their nuclear arsenals by a specified date, because of the impossibility of knowing whether security and other conditions will be satisfactory at a particular point in the future. But as a general matter, India seems the most willing of all nuclear-armed states to participate in the global elimination of nuclear arsenals.

Pakistan

Pakistan is estimated to possess roughly 60 nuclear weapons.[19] It continues to expand its capacity to produce fissile material for weapons and to improve its land-based ballistic missiles, its favoured means of delivery. Like India, Pakistan is expected to develop the capability to deploy cruise missiles. Pakistan explicitly allows the possibility of using nuclear weapons first in a conflict. This reflects the basic fact that Pakistan acquired and maintains nuclear weapons to compensate for India's overall strategic advantages. While Pakistan's leaders have sought and won domestic popularity through the prowess symbolised by nuclear weapons, they would find it difficult to resist a global movement to abolish nuclear weapons if India were similarly committed, and if China and the US – Pakistan's most important backers – were too. Pakistan's abiding interest in protecting its territorial integrity and political autonomy from Indian coercion would, however, require that India agree to conventional arms-control and confidence-building measures. As discussed below, these would not be easy measures to design.

Israel

Israel has long said that it 'would not be the first to introduce nuclear weapons to the Middle East', a formulation interpreted to mean that it would only contemplate using nuclear weapons after an adversary had 'introduced' them by posing an imminent nuclear threat to Israel. Israeli leaders from all the major political parties have been remarkably restrained and consistent in their treatment of the nuclear issue, not brandishing the country's nuclear weapons for political gain or to intimidate adversaries. Nuclear weapons are kept in the background of both domestic and regional politics. Estimates of Israel's actual holdings vary widely, primarily because the state does not acknowledge possession of nuclear weapons and retains exceptionally tight secrecy over this domain. The country is believed to possess sophisticated nuclear warheads with a range of yields, and it has aircraft, land-based missiles and, most importantly, submarines with which it could deliver nuclear weapons to any of its likely adversaries.

Israel has signed the CTBT and has advocated an open-ended verifiable moratorium on testing, pending entry into force of the treaty. It has said that it will join a weapons-of-mass-destruction-free zone in the Middle East once all regional states, including Iran, establish a durable peace with it and are sufficiently transparent to accept and implement a regionally controlled verification regime that includes mutual verification. Israel does not have confidence that a globally agreed verification regime with an international organisation such as the IAEA as its inspectorate would ensure that all nuclear, biological and chemical weapons had been eliminated from the Middle East, nor that rearmament would be detected in a timely enough fashion to enable Israel to respond effectively. Even if all other nuclear-armed states agreed to eliminate their nuclear arsenals, Israel would not join them unless political, security, verification and transparency conditions specific to the Middle East were to its satisfaction. Conversely, however, this does mean that Israel might conceivably eliminate its nuclear arsenal independently of the full disarmament of the other nuclear-armed states, if its security requirements in the Middle East were met (which would include a ban on indigenous nuclear-fuel-cycle facilities in the region).

The first hurdles

Conventional-force balances

Early on in an arms-reduction process, Russia and China would want to be persuaded that the relative power of the US would not increase under a prohibition of nuclear weapons. Many other states would share their concern. There is tension between the US interest in and obligation to use its power to defend international norms and its allies and friends, and the concerns that other states have about US military power projection and interventionism. Reassurance from the US that a world without nuclear weapons would not increase the threat of US interventions need not be a precondition for taking many steps towards nuclear disarmament, but Russia and China would be more halting participants to the degree that such reassurance was not provided.

Former US Secretary of Defense Harold Brown has written recently that 'US conventional power-projection capability and the concern that it may be used to intimidate, attack, or overthrow regimes' elevates interest in nuclear weapons as equalisers and deterrents of US conventional power.[20] The goal and project of prohibiting nuclear weapons cannot eliminate or sublimate power balancing, which is an enduring feature of international relations. An eventual nuclear-abolition project could only succeed if it were accompanied by changes in broader military relations that convinced states that now rely on nuclear deterrence that nuclear weapons would not be necessary to deter large-scale military interventions. For such changes to occur in the foreseeable future, the US would probably need to reassure others that it would abide by international law as understood by other major powers in determining whether, when and how to use military force. It would be unnecessary, unrealistic and unfair to expect the US and its supporters to forsake moral purpose in their foreign policies; military intervention can be necessary to prevent or end egregious violations of international laws and norms. But in order to persuade others to put down their nuclear arms and enforce a prohibition on nuclear weapons, the US would have to display a willingness to eschew unilateral or small-coalition military intervention for these purposes. Otherwise, an interest in balancing and deterring overall US military power would make retention of nuclear weapons feel imperative, especially to Russia and China.

Conventional arms-control and confidence-building measures would probably need to be implemented in the regions abutting Russia and China, and in South Asia. Russia and NATO have negotiated such arrangements in the past, and China and Russia have undertaken military confidence-building in the context of establishing the Shanghai Cooperation Organisation. These arrangements would need to be built upon and extended, especially as China's overall power grows, thereby heightening the security concerns of Japan, Russia and China's other neighbours. Japan, Russia and others would need to be reassured that China's power-projection capabilities would not lead to coercion, and that the US would retain the means and will to help them balance China. Russia and China might need to buttress their conventional power to balance that of the US and to fill in the gaps projected to be left by the absence of nuclear deterrence, which might impel their neighbours in turn to augment their non-nuclear military power.

Russia, China and other states considering relinquishing nuclear weapons would probably seek agreed limits on US non-nuclear military capabilities. There are few, if any, precedents for such limits, as US conventional military power is based as much on quality as it is on quantity. The capabilities that most concern Russia and China derive in large part from information-acquisition and processing technologies, often involving space-based assets, which enable the US to deliver air attacks with great speed and precision. These capabilities are judged by some to be potentially overwhelming. As US strategy analyst Larry Wortzel has noted, Chinese military thinkers 'fear that a conventional [US] attack on China's strategic missile forces could render China vulnerable and leave it without a deterrent'.[21] Arms control traditionally operates on quantitative principles – weapons that can be counted, stacked against their counterparts and then verifiably withdrawn under agreed ratios. But the US military's 'revolution in military affairs' has introduced huge qualitative variables into balance-of-power calculations. The world has no experience of negotiating limits of the complexity that would be required for US qualitative advantages to be taken into account, even if the US were willing to entertain them. As and when political relations between major powers – in particular the US, Russia and China – become more cooperative, the daunting challenge of allaying concerns about the offensive potential of US military power could be taken up.[22] In the nearer term, unofficial analytical communities should lead the way in exploring these issues.

Finally, however, concerns about strategic intentions and conventional force imbalances in a nuclear-disarmed world should not be allowed to justify any US or Russian refusals to reduce nuclear arsenals to low numbers, or a Chinese nuclear build-up – in the event that the ballistic-missile defence problem, treated below, were resolved. As long as each state had survivable nuclear forces capable of threatening each other's capitals and leadership centres (which could not count on immunity even under doctrines prohibiting the deliberate targeting of civilians), conventional-force imbalances need not be less bearable than they have been historically. Indeed, the implementation of nuclear-arms control and reduction measures by the US, Russia and China – short of going from low numbers to zero – could make the political climate more conducive to the cooperative management of conventional military dynamics.

Ballistic-missile defence

Ballistic-missile defences will inescapably influence the prospects of further nuclear reductions and eventually of prohibiting nuclear weapons. If reliable testing convinces impartial observers that ballistic-missile defences would be highly effective in real-world scenarios, this technology could make nuclear disarmament more feasible, by insuring against the risk of cheating and nuclear threats involving low numbers of weapons. Effective missile defences could also reassure disarming nuclear states about the risk of conventional attack involving ballistic missiles. In each scenario, ballistic-missile defences could help both to counter an important threat and to deter it in the first place. (This would be true whether or not ballistic missiles were banned as part of a regime to eliminate nuclear weapons).

However, as long as the US, Russia and China have no shared conception of whether and how they might regulate their competition in strategic weaponry, the deployment of ballistic-missile defences increases rather than decreases the salience of nuclear weapons. This is due to the risk that the possession of such defences might embolden a state to launch a nuclear or conventional first strike against an adversary's nuclear forces, in the belief that it could then use its ballistic-missile defences to block a retaliatory salvo from whatever forces survived the attack. Even if a state with such defences had no intention of launching any such first strike, other states could not be sure of this.

In a situation in which Russia and China still fear that the US (and each other) could threaten their core security interests, the more extensive and effective ballistic-missile defences are, the less likely these countries will be to reduce their offensive nuclear systems to low levels. Similar calculations would take place in Pakistan if India acquired ballistic-missile defences. The US, Russia and China – and, therefore, the world – would not transition to very small nuclear arsenals, let alone none, if they did not first develop a cooperative approach to ballistic-missile defence, which in turn would require cooperation in managing their offensive strategic forces. Opinion leaders and policymakers from other countries could play an important role in impressing upon these states that the shared goal of implementing a more secure global nuclear order requires them to seriously explore whether and how ballistic-missile-defence deployment can be reconciled with strategic stability.

Regional nuclear powers, unsettled sovereignty and big-power projection
The eight nuclear-armed states will not be able to collectively envisage a prohibition of nuclear weapons until conflicts centring on Taiwan, Kashmir, Palestine and (perhaps) the Russian periphery are resolved, or at least durably stabilised. These are questions of unsettled sovereignty involving states that regard them as essentially internal disputes and which retain

nuclear weapons, at least in part, to prevent them from being settled by force against their interests. China insists that Taiwan is an internal affair. India does not accept that Kashmir is a matter for international resolution. Russia's periphery contains pockets of separatism that could produce conflict between Russia and other states that Russia would insist, rightly or wrongly, should not be considered matters of international peace and security. Israel – in common with rejectionist Arab states, Iran and, indeed, the wider international community – has not yet recognised Palestine as a separate state.

If these sovereignty disputes are resolved, it will be by those directly involved, not by outside actors. Nuclear weapons help to ensure that this is the case, by enabling their possessors to deter others from imposing unacceptable outcomes. Once any resolution were achieved, states would want to mobilise outside power, perhaps through the UN Security Council, to help maintain an agreed status quo and restore it if it were broken.

There is some cause for optimism that the Kashmir and Taiwan impediments to nuclear disarmament could be removed in the coming years. India and Pakistan have recently worked to stabilise their relations and identify ways to pacify, if not resolve, the Kashmir dispute. India has traditionally been more prepared to formally accept the status quo in Kashmir than has Pakistan. But the new military leadership of Pakistan under Army Chief of Staff General Ashfaq Kiyani shows signs of recognising that the country's greatest security imperative is to combat the operation of those prosecuting terrorism and violence against the state and civilians. This is related to the problem of extending central governance to the Federally Administered Tribal Areas and stabilising the porous border between these areas and Afghanistan. To the extent that the Pakistani Army and security services concentrate their activities on addressing these largely internal challenges and diminish the historic obsession with confronting India in Kashmir, Indo-Pakistani relations could be normalised, and a formal peace negotiated. Such an outcome is far from clear, but its prospect is better than it has been in decades. As and when the two South Asian powers formally stabilise their security relationship, the possibility of their negotiating nuclear-arms control and further confidence-building measures will become real.

China's growing wealth and power make seeking a breach through formal independence an increasingly unattractive option for Taiwan. This was reflected by the victory of the Nationalist Party in the Taiwanese elections of March 2008, the leader of which, Ma Ying-jeou, had campaigned on rapprochement with Beijing, and by the ensuing tentative moves made by China and Taiwan to build mutual confidence. As memories of 1949 fade and the challenges of peacefully managing Sino-American relations rise, US leaders have become clearer that Washington's obligations to Taiwan hold only so long as the island does not provoke conflict by declaring independence.[23] If this position gains even more political traction in the US, it could facilitate arms control between the US and China (and therefore Russia) and increase stability. The point here is not to predict such a development, but rather to acknowledge that Chinese officials will regard it as necessary if China is to agree steps to limit and eventually forgo its reliance on nuclear weapons.

Tensions between Russia, its smaller neighbours and national enclaves within them are more fluid and less difficult to resolve than Taiwan or Kashmir. For Russia to diminish its recently increased emphasis on nuclear forces, the US and NATO would need to demonstrate greater sensitivity to Russian concerns about ballistic-missile defence and interference in its periphery. At the same time, the US and NATO have political and moral interests in not leaving newly independent states on Russia's periphery vulnerable to Russian coercion and interference in their internal affairs. Washington has found it difficult to prioritise what it seeks from Russia – further nuclear reductions, closer cooperation on inducing Iran to comply with UN Security Council resolutions, greater respect for civil rights within Russia and non-interference in Georgia and Ukraine jostle among the US's demands and aspirations. If the international community wants the nuclear-arms-reduction and disarmament process to be intensified, it could contribute by urging Washington and Moscow to prioritise reaching better mutual understanding on these and other issues.

The ongoing Palestinian crisis and its effects on Israel's security calculations and Iran's foreign policy give less cause for optimism. This web of challenges need not paralyse efforts to move in other regions and globally to reduce the numbers and salience of nuclear weapons. However, the realisation of later steps towards a prohibition of nuclear weapons would not be feasible without breakthroughs in the willingness of Israel, Palestinians and rejectionist states to establish a reliable modus vivendi.

There is significant interaction between these regional dynamics, the wider global order and prospects for advancing towards nuclear abolition. The United States is the primary link. It features among the security concerns of actors in each of the regional clusters in which new balances will be necessary to induce states to reduce and subsequently eliminate their nuclear armouries. The US is key in the China–Taiwan scenario. It also has the responsibility for reassuring Japan in the face of growing

Chinese power. Russia will be interested in eliciting reassurances about US competition on its periphery and US conventional and space power – reassurances which Washington cannot easily provide to the extent that it also seeks to protect the interests of Russia's neighbours. In the Middle East, US military capabilities at least partly inform the military policies of Iran, Syria and others that Israel must balance. Washington also provides conventional military reassurance to Egypt, Jordan and the Gulf Cooperation Council states.

In South Asia, the appearance of a strategic partnership between the US and India, including on ballistic-missile defence, advanced conventional weaponry and civilian space and nuclear technology, affects the calculations of Pakistan and China. Even without US backing, India's growing conventional military advantages induce Pakistan to place higher value on nuclear deterrence. Pakistan would probably seek limits on Indian conventional power before it would agree to reduce its nuclear arsenal. India, in turn, would point to its need to balance both Pakistani and Chinese military power, greatly complicating the task of both nuclear and conventional arms control.

Extended deterrence

Recent US discussions of the importance of seeking a world free of nuclear weapons have elicited intense, albeit quietly expressed, concern that this prospect could encourage nuclear proliferation by casting doubt on the viability of extended deterrence, that is, on the commitments made by Washington to project its military power to deter aggression against its allies and friends. Most prominently, it has been suggested that Japan might reconsider its commitment not to develop nuclear weapons because of a fear that US extended deterrence might be withdrawn.[24] (Turkey is also frequently cited in this regard.) The reasons for this are not immediately clear. The US would only eliminate its last nuclear weapons at the same time as all other actors, including China, eliminated theirs, with verification and enforcement provisions negotiated to all states' satisfaction. In this scenario, the nuclear threats against which the US currently provides an umbrella nuclear deterrent would have been removed. The US would presumably maintain its security commitments to allies and be prepared to meet these commitments with conventional means. The conventional balancing requirement could be met by building up US and Japanese capabilities to substitute for the loss of nuclear deterrence – assuming this were still necessary in the absence of Chinese nuclear weapons – or by conventional arms control.

The real concern seems to be less about the end state than about the process of moving from today's strategic environment to one without nuclear weapons. That is, if the US were now to evince a clear interest in global prohibition of nuclear weapons, Japan or other US allies might conclude that the US would be unwilling to stand by its extended nuclear deterrent commitments in the decades-long transition to nuclear abolition. In this period, China (and perhaps North Korea) would retain nuclear weapons, and Japanese security officials might judge that Washington would be unwilling to risk nuclear conflict to deter them from coercing Japan. Japan might then seek nuclear weapons to secure itself during an uncertain transition to a nuclear-weapons-free world. This might in turn motivate South Korea to hedge or break its non-proliferation commitment. A similar scenario could be imagined in regard to Turkey, especially if Iran were to acquire a capability to produce nuclear weapons and NATO had attenuated its commitment and/or capacity to extend nuclear deterrence to its members.

While these concerns cannot be dismissed out of hand, the risk that countries that now enjoy an extended deterrent would be left vulnerable on the way to abolition must not be exaggerated. The most immediate need is to reassure states that value American and NATO extended nuclear deterrence that decisions regarding nuclear forces will not be made over their heads. The Japanese government and public strongly support the objective of nuclear disarmament, even as they value extended nuclear deterrence so long as nuclear weapons exist. The Turkish government, too, advocates nuclear disarmament. The nuclear-armed allies of these states, especially the US, would be irresponsible and ineffective if they did not involve them in deliberations on the step-by-step processes that could reduce global nuclear arsenals from current levels to zero. These steps will need to address the issues of conventional-force balancing, regional confidence-building and ballistic-missile defence discussed above. If China, Russia, North Korea, Iran and others do not cooperate in reducing insecurities surrounding the states that now benefit from extended nuclear deterrence, the US, as the principal guarantor, would not and should not be expected to relinquish this deterrent. Moreover, as China's decision to press North Korea to agree to denuclearise appears to indicate, the prospect of Japanese and/or South Korean nuclear armament may in fact be motivating Chinese cooperation on reducing such insecurities. Such cooperation should lessen proliferation risks.

Extended deterrence is among the political–security issues that would need to be addressed on the way to the horizon from which the feasibility of a global prohibition of nuclear weapons could be seriously explored.

Like the issues of verification and the management of nuclear industry discussed in subsequent chapters, decisions regarding extended deterrence would require the active participation of non-nuclear-weapons states. This is yet another way in which nuclear abolition is not simply a challenge for the nuclear-armed states.

Nuclear terrorism

The threat of nuclear terrorism elicits much fear today, especially in the US, the UK, France, Russia, India and Israel. This fear increases resistance to taking nuclear disarmament seriously, though it ought to be irrelevant to decisions about dramatically reducing the number and salience of nuclear weapons. It should be evident that retaining nuclear weapons is unnecessary and not helpful for pre-empting, deterring or retaliating against nuclear terrorism.

The most effective way to prevent nuclear terrorism is to ensure that fissile materials or nuclear weapons cannot be obtained by terrorist organisations. Terrorist groups are highly unlikely to be able to produce fissile materials themselves. The US and the G8 have established and funded important initiatives to improve the security of nuclear materials, and the IAEA and other nuclear-industry organisations are contributing to these and other nuclear-security schemes. The Global Initiative to Combat Nuclear Terrorism, led by the US and Russia, now includes 70 partner states committed to improving accounting, control and physical-protection systems for nuclear materials, enhancing the security of civilian nuclear facilities and taking other measures to prevent nuclear terrorism.

To the extent that the risk of fissile-material diversion grows as the number of states and facilities producing the material increases, the world needs to adopt new rules to prevent the spread of weapons-usable fissile material production capabilities to additional states. This issue is discussed in detail elsewhere in this paper. For now, it is important to note that taking nuclear abolition more seriously could help to overcome the resistance that key non-nuclear-weapons states have mounted to tightening rules on the spread of fuel-cycle capabilities.

States with nuclear weapons still need to be convinced, however, that these weapons are not necessary deterrents against nuclear and biological terrorism. Officials in the US, France, Russia, India and Israel have all at times identified state sponsorship of nuclear and biological terrorism among the threats their nuclear forces are supposed to deter.

There is very good reason to doubt that nuclear weapons could either deter or pre-empt a nuclear or biological terrorist attack. A nuclear attack on terrorists would be difficult to successfully carry out. The central challenge in targeting terrorists is to locate them; no weapon, nuclear or otherwise, is useful if it cannot be directed to the relevant target. If terrorists can be located with the confidence and precision that would be required to justify using nuclear weapons against them, it is likely that other means of destruction could be effectively deployed, with less collateral damage. The Iraq War vividly illustrates the primacy of intelligence over ordnance in targeting terrorists. Of the 50 aerial strikes US forces mounted on Iraqi leaders in 2003, not one resulted in the death of the intended target, according to an exhaustive Human Rights Watch investigation.[25] However, many untargeted people were killed. The extremely poor record of targeting and killing individual leaders with missile or manned-aircraft strikes would make any US president highly unlikely to authorise using nuclear weapons in this role, as US military officials privately recognise.

It is suggested that the threat of nuclear strikes against states and societies that might aid or harbour nuclear terrorists could motivate these states and societies to expel any terrorists they were protecting. Yet this is a complicated problem, as can be seen from efforts to expel al-Qaeda from Afghanistan, Pakistan, Iraq and Iran. Even when political leaders wish to eliminate terrorists from their midst, their capacity to do so is uncertain. Threatening to use nuclear weapons against such states is fraught with moral, political and strategic problems that make the threat highly counterproductive, as well as not particularly credible. For example, were the US or Israel to threaten to use nuclear weapons against states found to be harbouring nuclear terrorists, this could intensify popular animus against the US and Israel, and against governments that were seen as being complicit with them, to the possible gain of terrorist causes.

Other strategic problems arise from threatening nuclear retaliation against states from which terrorists might acquire fissile materials or weapons. To be able to identify the sponsors of nuclear terrorists, targeted countries such as the US, France or the UK would need to develop the forensic capacity to identify the sources of nuclear materials and weapons used by terrorists. This would require the cooperation of the states that now possess such materials. Samples would be needed to create databases against which to compare the nuclear 'fingerprints' of a terrorist bomb. In the event of a nuclear terrorist attack, more intense cooperation with potential source states would be needed. The highest priority would be cooperation to prevent subsequent attacks. Yet if the US or other nuclear-armed states had declared their willingness to mount nuclear counter-strikes against source countries, those countries might be less willing to cooperate, either before or after an attack. Would a state provide information for a nuclear-fingerprint database, for example, if it knew that the US could use this information as a reason for striking it with nuclear weapons? These issues need to be explored now, and in the process it will become clearer to what extent nuclear counter-threats are an obstacle to cooperation on combating nuclear terrorism. In conducting such explorations, it would be wise to also consider whether cooperation would be more or less likely if the major nuclear powers were explicitly seeking to take steps towards a world without nuclear weapons.

The next steps

Transparency as an early step?
Nuclear-armed states are often urged to declare precisely how many nuclear weapons they hold, how many they have produced, how much fissile material they retain, and so on. In March 2008, French President Sarkozy invited 'the five nuclear-weapon states recognised by the NPT to agree on transparency measures'.[26]

A brief exploration of this issue reveals that key states and regions have more work to do to establish security relationships conducive to transparency. Because China retains a nuclear arsenal much smaller than that of Russia or the US, it relies on secrecy regarding the size and disposition of this arsenal to help protect its survivability. China perceives that the US has not clearly accepted a relationship of mutual deterrence with it. That is to say, the US has not reassured China that it will not seek or use military capabilities to negate China's capacity to retaliate with nuclear weapons against any US first strike. The US may know that China has a small arsenal, but if it does not know the exact number and location of weapons capable of threatening US targets, Washington cannot be sure that it could destroy them all in a first strike. Beijing can therefore have some confidence that Washington believes China could destroy an American city or two in retaliation, and hence that the US would be unlikely to risk major warfare with a nuclear attack, for example in any conflict over Taiwan. If, by contrast, the US were certain about China's inventory, Chinese authorities might conclude that they needed to build a larger and more readily launchable arsenal than they now plan. In addition, the uncertainties around US ballistic-missile-defence plans mean that the Chinese authorities are reluctant to declare their holdings of fissile materials or any upper limits they might envisage for their nuclear forces. However, there is an important distinction to be drawn between capabilities and doctrine. None of the above considerations need prevent greater Chinese transparency about doctrine, which is particularly desirable in view of the ongoing questioning by some Chinese military strategists of the wisdom of adhering to China's no-first-use doctrine in any confrontation with the US over Taiwan.[27]

Pakistan and India both rely on secrecy to augment their nuclear deterrents and limit domestic political pressure to build larger and more costly stockpiles and arsenals. Each hopes that secrecy about the size and location of its nuclear arsenal will keep adversaries from concluding that they could successfully target these capabilities. Keeping adversaries guessing is a way of reducing vulnerability to a first strike, and of thereby easing internal pressure to build larger retaliatory forces operating at higher launch readiness. Opacity about stocks of fissile material provides decision-makers in both states with greater freedom to determine how much is enough. If, for example, Pakistan were to declare an inventory of separated plutonium and highly enriched uranium larger than India's, Indian public opinion might express surprise and concern, and be liable to demand that the government hurriedly expand production.

Modification of Israel's nuclear-opacity policy would have several security implications. It seems clear that if Israel unambiguously announced its possession of nuclear weapons, pressure would grow within Egypt, Iran and other states to ramp up countervailing capabilities. If, in the absence of a verifiable and enforceable agreement to bring about a WMD-free zone in the Middle East, Israel declared how much fissile material it had produced outside international safeguards, domestic pressure could mount on Arab governments and Iran to begin producing fissile material under safeguards. Even if this material were put to purely peaceful uses, its production could well be perceived in the region as a hedge to keep the nuclear-weapons option open, and hence be destabilising.

The reasons for some states' reluctance to become much more transparent about their nuclear holdings need to be addressed, ultimately through conflict resolution and reciprocal confidence-building measures of the kinds discussed above. Yet these concerns should not keep officials and experts in states and international bodies from devising transparency measures that could be effective in the event that the political will emerges to enhance nuclear transparency at regional and/or global levels. Nor is there any reason for Russia and the US not to become more transparent now, including about the inventories and disposition of their 'non-strategic' nuclear weapons, that is, weapons – generally of smaller yields – designed for battlefield use. Transparency measures could be invaluable precursors to an eventual nuclear-disarmament agreement that would require full disclosure of all production and holdings of nuclear weapons and fissile materials.[28]

One way to test the willingness of the US, Russia, China, India, Pakistan, Israel and others to move ahead on nuclear disarmament, and to elaborate the conditions that must be established for them to be able to do this, would be to elicit and discuss their officials' private objections to nuclear transparency. No forum or process has been established to do this discreetly. The long-running discussions in the Conference on Disarmament of a possible treaty to ban unsafeguarded fissile-material production are not conducive to the candour we invite here. An alternative would be for the eight states that have legitimately produced fissile materials outside international safeguards to create a working group on transparency, as part of a good-faith effort to show the rest of the world that they are prepared to take nuclear disarmament seriously.

Further preliminary steps

Many of the measures discussed in the preceding paragraphs and in ensuing chapters on verification, nuclear-industry management and enforcement would be invaluable both to strengthening protections against proliferation and to facilitating nuclear disarmament. Here we discuss several other steps, each constructive in its own right, that would be beneficial for states to take at an early stage. It will be necessary for some of these to be taken in order that the more far-reaching political and security conditions for the total elimination of nuclear arsenals can come about.

North Korea must cease to pose a nuclear-weapons threat if the legitimate possessors of nuclear weapons are to look over today's horizon and imagine that the elimination of all nuclear arsenals could be feasible. A framework, albeit an uncertain one, exists for North Korea's nuclear disarmament. The immediate challenge is implementation. North Korea has recently declared its plutonium holdings and production history, and talks are currently under way to agree on the details of verification. In the longer term North Korea's suspected efforts to enrich uranium and its nuclear cooperation with Syria will have to be addressed. It must also declare its nuclear-weapons facilities and the weapons themselves.

The process of disclosure will be a complicated one that could serve as a test laboratory for future disarmament-verification processes elsewhere. Even if North Korea were to convince the other participants in the Six-Party Talks that it was providing them with all the information it possessed, there might be discrepancies between its records, the physical evidence and other parties' intelligence estimates. In particular, building confidence in North Korea's claims about the quantities of plutonium lost during reprocessing[29] and used in its October 2006 nuclear test presents a significant challenge, as there is no easy way of verifying the former quantity and it is impossible to verify the latter. North Korea therefore presents a useful opportunity for demonstrating whether such challenges, which will inevitably arise in the course of attempts to verify disarmament (discussed further in the following chapter), can be resolved successfully. Indeed, given that plutonium production is more susceptible to physical verification than is highly-enriched-uranium (HEU) production, success in verifiably disarming North Korea is vital if the abolition of all nuclear weapons is to be taken seriously.

Differences among North Korea's interlocutors could arise in negotiations, and it is not immediately evident how these would be resolved. Participants should remember, however, that a constructive agreement on a verification process for North Korea is valuable, not only for its immediate contributions to alleviating nuclear insecurity, but also for its use as a test case for future nuclear disarmament. Needless to say, if North Korea refuses to cooperate, either in disclosing its nuclear record or, most importantly, in dismantling all of its weapons and related production capability, this would set a floor below which the other nuclear-weapons states would not reduce their own arsenals.

The case of Iran tests a number of parts of the international system that must be strengthened to build confidence that regional and global nuclear-weapons prohibitions would be feasible. Iran was caught violating its IAEA safeguards agreement. The detection system worked in time, before Iran acquired fissile materials or nuclear weapons. The responsible enforcement authorities were summoned. They ordered Iran to freeze – to stop its suspicious, potentially threatening activities until their peaceful nature could be established and confidence in Iran's intentions restored. But six years after its clandestine activities were discovered, Iran is still staring down the enforcement authorities – the IAEA board of governors and the UN Security Council – having defiantly taken steps that it was expressly ordered not to. If Iran continues to successfully defy the rules, procedures and enforcement authorities of the nuclear non-proliferation regime, there is no reason for anyone to have confidence that rules to guide and secure a nuclear-weapons-free world would be enforced.

Some will argue that Iran is motivated to continue its defiance, and other states are inclined to tolerate it, because the US, Israel and others possess nuclear weapons. The nuclear 'double standard' is said to explain or excuse Iran's interest in obtaining nuclear-weapons capabilities. It is certainly possible that if no one else possessed nuclear weapons, Iran would be more cooperative and the international community more insistent.

But Iranian leaders insist that they do not seek nuclear weapons, and they have not said that the existence of nuclear weapons elsewhere is what motivates them to continue enrichment. Nor do they justify their refusal to comply with legally binding Security Council resolutions in these terms.

The Iran case is deeply damaging to the objective of global nuclear disarmament. A party to the NPT that has broken its safeguards agreement and failed to cooperate with the IAEA to resolve all outstanding questions regarding the exclusively peaceful nature of its nuclear activities is defying the proper enforcement mechanisms of the non-proliferation regime. If and when Iran fully complies with these mechanisms, this would be the time to negotiate adjustments to the non-proliferation regime to prevent future violations and to address the 'double standards' criticism.

Global nuclear abolition cannot happen without the simultaneous or prior establishment of a verifiable WMD-free zone in the Middle East. Iran's refusal to comply with IAEA and Security Council obligations renders both objectives impossible. Israel's possession of nuclear weapons does too. But Iran, unlike Israel, blocks even the first steps towards creating such a zone by not recognising Israel's right to exist. It is politically unrealistic to expect a state to relinquish its nuclear deterrent as long as its neighbours and declared adversaries do not recognise its existence or demonstrate the political will to live in peace with it. Indeed, Iran's belligerent attitude towards Israel and its support of organisations that practise terrorism is a major reason why the international community is so troubled by its operation of facilities that could produce nuclear-weapons fuel. The removal of this apparent threat is a necessary political and security precondition for allowing evolutionary steps towards regional and global nuclear disarmament.

Regardless of developments in Iran and North Korea, the international community could demonstrate its willingness to begin making the changes necessary to facilitate nuclear disarmament by making the illicit proliferation of nuclear weapons an international crime. Slavery, piracy and hijacking are international crimes today, but the proliferation of nuclear weapons is not. UN Security Council Resolution 1540 obliges all states to adopt national legislation to prevent and criminalise the proliferation of nuclear-weapons capabilities to non-state actors. (Several states – including Pakistan, which continues to rely on imports to improve its nuclear deterrent – ensured that proliferation to *states* was not covered by the resolution.) Making proliferation to non-state actors an international crime would diminish the risk that proliferation networks would thrive in states with lax enforcement of national laws. Such networks could serve not only terrorists but also states that aspired to break their non-proliferation obligations and acquire nuclear-weapons capabilities. Under such a law, proliferators would be subject to arrest and prosecution anywhere in the world. States that did not support this international legal buttressing of commitments already made under Resolution 1540 would reveal their real, as opposed to rhetorical, attitudes toward nuclear disarmament.

States that possess nuclear weapons could quickly and importantly build confidence by altering the operational postures of their nuclear forces and by making them less salient in their national-security doctrines. Here India, Pakistan and Israel offer relatively positive models. Pakistan, as well as India, refrains from deploying nuclear weapons mated with their delivery systems, and neither country's force is poised for rapid launch. They are thus less susceptible to accidental use. Israel does not rattle nuclear sabres to gratify a domestic audience, assert its status or intimidate other states. The nuclear-armed states as a group would do much to reassure the world if they adopted a standard whereby they did not routinely deploy nuclear weapons poised for immediate use and vulnerable to destruction if not used upon warning of an incoming attack. This is primarily an issue for the US and Russia, but it should also be a general principle that no national leader should be in the position of feeling they must unleash the destructive power of nuclear weapons immediately upon warning of attack, or risk losing their state's capacity to retaliate.

In previous discussions of the desirability and feasibility of nuclear disarmament, experts in states with nuclear weapons have predicted that, as the big nuclear powers reduce their arsenals to low numbers, states that do not now possess nuclear weapons might become tempted to acquire them.[30] At the stage where the largest arsenals numbered weapons in the low hundreds, the argument goes, an upstart possessor of nuclear weapons could believe that it had the opportunity to rise dramatically in the international nuclear ranks. This possibility cannot be dismissed, but it should not be seen as a barrier to disarmament. Reduction to relatively small arsenals would be part of an evolutionary process that states could readily halt or reverse if new actors sought nuclear weapons. In any case, if much increased collective confidence in the enforceability of strengthened non-proliferation rules is not achieved, the current nuclear-armed states will not undertake reductions to numbers so low as to invite, in their view, new proliferation. Moreover, an aspiring nuclear-armed power would need to weigh the political and strategic gains it hoped to make against risks and costs of proliferation that presumably would be much greater than in today's world. The proliferator would be breaking a truly global anti-nuclear-weapons norm, rather than seeking to join a handful of nuclear-weapons possessors in a divided, inequitable nuclear order of 'haves' and 'have-nots'. In other words, the political, economic and security barriers to nuclear armament would be high enough to outweigh any hoped-for gains to be made from seeking to balance the arsenals of states moving towards zero.

It is likely that the more serious 'low numbers' issue would be that the possessors of nuclear weapons would prefer to stop at a plateau of small nuclear forces rather than take on the perceived added risks and costs of going to zero. The nuclear-armed states might be tempted to try to make a new bargain with non-nuclear-weapons states, in which the radically reduced political and military salience and numbers of nuclear weapons would be sufficient to enable the adoption and robust enforcement of a stronger non-proliferation regime – the outcome that primarily motivates whatever interest nuclear-armed states currently have in nuclear disarmament. The question would then become whether leading non-nuclear-weapons states would be willing to negotiate and implement such a revised bargain.

The challenge of achieving stability and security in a world with much greater nuclear parity at much lower total numbers should be addressed sooner rather than later to demonstrate a serious interest in nuclear disarmament. Official and unofficial experts should be encouraged on an international basis to model this problem.

CHAPTER TWO

Verifying the Transition to Zero

The politics of verifying disarmament

Verification serves a number of functions in any arms-reduction process. It helps to build confidence that states are abiding by the terms of an agreement. By detecting non-compliance, it acts as a trigger for enforcement actions, and is therefore also a deterrent. Without strong verification provisions, it is difficult to generate political will among states to give up military capabilities.

Although non-nuclear-weapons states generally acknowledge the role of verification, there may well be a divergence of views among them about exactly how important it is. States, such as Japan and South Korea, that have chosen to rely on the US nuclear umbrella to counterbalance a nuclear-armed neighbour, would be apt to insist upon particularly high standards of verification. A majority of non-nuclear-weapons states might well not require the same standard of verification, concluding that any uncertainties would leave them not significantly worse off than they are in today's world laden with nuclear weapons.

Nuclear-armed states are not likely to share this perspective. Their security interests and responsibilities, historical experiences and socio-political acculturation to possessing nuclear weapons may make them disinclined to accept the material and political uncertainties outlined in the following discussion. Almost certainly, politically significant elements within these states would demand 'perfect' verification as a condition for supporting (and ratifying) a prohibition of nuclear weapons.[1]

Would 'perfect' verification be necessary?

Speaking before the US Senate Foreign Relations Committee during its hearings on the 1987 Intermediate Nuclear Forces (INF) Treaty, Ambassador Paul Nitze stated that an effective verification system must be able to detect a violation in which a party 'moved beyond the limits of the treaty in a *militarily significant* way'. For example, in the case of the SS-20, a mobile intermediate-range ballistic missile banned under the INF treaty, the threshold for military significance was set at about 50 missiles.[2] In practical terms, this meant that when the US attempted to verify Soviet compliance with the treaty, it put in sufficient inspection effort to assure itself that the Soviet Union had fewer than 50 SS-20s left. As the most common version of the SS-20 (the Mod 2) had three re-entry vehicles, this could have amounted to up to 150 warheads. Verifying to the same degree of confidence that the Soviet Union had dismantled all its SS-20s would have required more overflights and inspections and been correspondingly more expensive.

No verification system is designed to detect arbitrarily small treaty violations (whether or not they are intentional). But what constitutes a militarily significant violation depends on the context. Had the US and the Soviet Union possessed fewer nuclear weapons of other types when the INF treaty was concluded, verification of SS-20s would probably have needed to be more stringent. Russia and the US have had very little incentive to cheat in the nuclear-arms reductions they have undertaken so far. Each country has possessed such large weapons and fissile-material stockpiles that there has been no motivation for secreting away a few weapons or kilogrammes of plutonium. There would have been little incentive to cheat even if there had been no risk of detection; with the risk of detection, the incentives have been strongly against cheating. And, partly because each side has retained assured nuclear retaliatory capability, the actual standard of verification required has been rather low.

In 1961, President Kennedy's science adviser, Jerome Wiesner, argued that as zero was approached, the quantity of undisclosed weapons or fissile materials that would be militarily significant would get progressively smaller.[3] This would increase the demands placed on verification. This argument is certainly intuitively appealing. In a transition from the last hundred or tens of weapons to zero, would not a state preparing to give up its nuclear deterrent be extremely concerned about any risk that others were cheating? Would not all states assume that others had incentives to cheat, at least to a much greater degree than under any arms-control treaty hitherto negotiated? Would not perfect, or at least

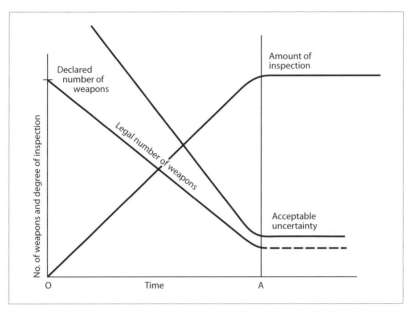

Figure 1: The 'Wiesner curve'. Based on figure 40 in Allan S. Krass, *Verification: How Much is Enough?* (London: Taylor and Francis for SIPRI, 1985), p. 168.

unattainably good, verification therefore be needed in the final transition to zero?

The so-called Wiesner curve (shown in Figure 1) might possibly be misleading for three reasons. Firstly, would the militarily significant quantity in a nuclear-weapons-free world actually be so small as to make verification unfeasible? Or, in plainer language, would a small cache of fissile materials or nuclear weapons, whether acquired by a 'rogue state' or a major power, really pose an unacceptable threat to international peace and security? Analysts have argued this point both ways.[4] We will not rehearse the arguments here, as what matters is the perceptions of states. Different states are likely to have different views on the significance of very low-numbers cheating.

Secondly, as US non-proliferation expert Allan Krass has observed, in Wiesner's analysis the 'level of distrust is implicitly assumed to remain constant during the disarmament process'.[5] If, as zero is approached, robust verification finds no unresolvable indications of possible cheating and states become convinced that each truly intends to fulfil the agreement, they might no longer require such stringent verification. US arms-control analyst Steve Fetter has suggested that verification might need to be most robust at the level of around 100 warheads.[6] If no evidence of cheating emerged, states might then have enough confidence to dismantle their last warheads without spiralling demands for verification. This argument hinges on the assumption that verification would promote confidence, not only that states were complying with the terms of a disarmament agreement, but also that they had the intention of continuing to do so. This assumption is lent some empirical support by the fact that the US and Russia time-limited the verification arrangements for two strategic arms control treaties (START I and the INF) that are of indefinite duration.[7]

Finally, the Wiesner model ignores the fact that verification is a means to an end, not an end in itself. The end is compliance, and enforcement mechanisms too must exist for compliance to be promoted. As we discuss in more depth in Chapter 4, effective enforcement mechanisms would still be crucial even if verification were perfect. Imperfections in any verification system could potentially be offset by more robust enforcement mechanisms.

These issues of verification standards and practices have not been explored extensively even among the nuclear-armed states, let alone between nuclear-armed and non-nuclear-armed states. Such explorations would need to be undertaken well before a prohibition on nuclear weapons were negotiated. This is a subject on which useful preliminary analysis and discussion could begin now, at both official and unofficial levels. The February 2008 UK proposal to enlist weapons laboratories from all NPT nuclear-weapons states in exploring such verification issues should be welcomed.[8]

The mechanics of verification

We turn now to the mechanics of verification; examining the technologies and procedures that could be available to verify a transition to zero, their deficiencies and the prospects for overcoming these deficiencies. Throughout this discussion, it is important to bear in mind the political context of verification described above. At one extreme, states could ultimately be satisfied with a 'do your best' approach to verification; at the other, they might demand a very high standard of proof. In the former scenario, the verification weaknesses we identify below would simply cease to be regarded as problems. In the latter, they would become significant obstacles to abolishing nuclear weapons if they could not be solved. Given the uncertainty about the standard of verification that would be required, taking disarmament seriously must involve examining the potential verification pitfalls. This discussion is intended to highlight the key challenges. It is not exhaustive; there are a number of important issues that limitations of space prevent us from exploring – not least the question of what body should be tasked with verifying disarmament. Should it be the IAEA, or should a new inspectorate be created especially for the purpose? Is an international organisation needed at all?

What is disarmament?
The phrase 'complete nuclear disarmament' encompasses a range of end states. At one extreme lies what might be termed the 'purist' view of disarmament.[9] In this view, the objectives of nuclear disarmament would be to securely eliminate nuclear weapons and, as far as possible, erase states' capabilities to produce them. Following dismantlement, the non-nuclear components of weapons would be destroyed. Fissile material would be placed under international safeguards and converted, as far as possible, into forms not usable in nuclear weapons. The facilities used to design, fabricate and maintain nuclear weapons would be demolished or, at least, completely reoriented to purposes unrelated to nuclear weapons.

The purist position rejects the possibility of deliberately preserving some form of nuclear-weapons-reconstitution capability to act as a hedge. This study does not, in part because some hedging capabilities would inevitably exist, at least while weapons and related infrastructure were being dismantled. For the sake of argument, however, the paper first considers disarmament from a broadly purist perspective. Then, in Chapter 5, hedging is examined.

A key challenge in defining the terms of an abolition agreement would relate to dual- and multi-use activities, materials and equipment. The political and economic issues involved mean that there is substantial potential for disagreement on these questions, even among purists. The problem of what civilian nuclear activities should be permitted in a disarmed world is addressed at length later in this paper. A brief exploration of two other dual- or multi-use issues – production facilities and delivery systems – should help to illustrate some of the difficulties.

Any nuclear-disarmament agreement would need to ensure that states' nuclear-weapons complexes were not being used for proscribed purposes, whether this were achieved by destroying them, mothballing them or converting them to legitimate uses. But how should the term 'nuclear-weapons complex' be defined? Clearly those facilities involved in the fabrication of weapons pits (the metallic cores of nuclear warheads) or the final assembly of warheads, for example, would require monitoring, but what about those involved in the production of non-nuclear components? For instance, plants that currently mould, press and shape high-explosive charges or manufacture electronic components for nuclear warheads could easily be used to produce components for other purposes, and in some cases already are.[10] Would these need to be monitored? If so, would monitoring be possible without compromising the secrecy of non-nuclear military programmes? Would plants that produce equipment or materials, such as lithium-6, used in the manufacturing of 'secondaries' (the components of thermonuclear warheads that produce energy through nuclear fusion) require monitoring?

Should a disarmament agreement outlaw some types of delivery vehicle? The most obvious target for such a ban would be the ballistic missile. Ballistic missiles can have long ranges and are very difficult to defend against. They are therefore the delivery vehicle *par excellence* for high-cost, high-impact munitions such as nuclear weapons. The consequences of break-out from a nuclear-weapons-free regime would be considerably aggravated if the state in question possessed ballistic missiles. From this perspective, there is a strong case for banning them. Indeed, Russia has recently proposed making global the bilateral 1987 INF treaty, which eliminated all US and Russian ground-launched missiles with ranges from 500km to 5,500km, and France has suggested a worldwide ban on all short- and intermediate-range ballistic missiles.

However, depending on the munitions technology available to a state, ballistic missiles can also be used to deliver conventional, chemical or biological weapons. A September 2007 survey by the Arms Control Association lists 32 states that are known or believed to possess ballistic missiles.[11] Would it be necessary for these states to give up their missiles to bring about a nuclear-weapons-free world? If so, would they be willing to do so? Would states that possess ballistic missiles, but not cruise missiles or advanced air forces, insist that their rivals agree to ban those delivery systems, as a matter of effective equity, in return for the banning of ballistic missiles?

The purpose of this exposition is not to argue that questions and problems such as these pose insurmountable obstacles to disarmament, but rather to show that there are real questions about the scope and obligations of a potential disarmament agreement. It also illustrates that at least some of these questions are not merely technical problems that can be delegated to specialists, but are strategic issues, in that they impact on states' security and economic interests.

Checking correctness: verifying what has been declared
i. Verifying the dismantling of warheads
A central aim of verification would be to ensure that states had put declared warheads, and their constituent components and materials,

beyond use. This requirement would represent a new departure for nuclear-arms-control treaties. Because of the difficulties involved in verifying the dismantlement of warheads – mainly due to national-security concerns about warhead inspection – treaties have to date focused almost exclusively on delivery vehicles and their launchers. Indeed, Article I of the NPT prohibits inspectors from viewing warheads directly unless they happen to have the appropriate security clearances, and from using many other verification techniques routinely used with other fissile materials. In the late 1990s, it appeared that the next US–Russia arms-control treaty, START III, would require the destruction of warheads, along with appropriate transparency measures. But START III was never concluded, and its place was taken by the 2002 Moscow Treaty, which contains no verification provisions and does not require warheads to be destroyed. Nonetheless, preparations for START III stimulated extensive and detailed research into how the destruction of warheads might be verified.

In the following paragraphs, a scheme for verifying the dismantlement of warheads is sketched out.[12] This picture might be termed the standard model, and it represents a rough consensus in the literature. There are of course numerous variations on this central theme, but few are radically different.

Firstly, states would be required to submit detailed 'baseline' declarations specifying the location, type and possibly the history of each warhead.[13] Warhead containers (such as transport canisters, re-entry vehicles and free-fall bomb cases) would be tagged with a unique identifier conceptually – and quite possibly practically – similar to a barcode. To verify that baseline declarations were correct, inspectors would be permitted to inspect a random sample of warhead containers to check that they matched the state's declaration – the larger the sample, the greater the confidence in the declaration. Inspectors would also be allowed to count the total number of warheads present at each declared site to ensure that none had been omitted from the declaration. Ideally, verification of deployed warheads would start at their deployment sites, so that a chain of custody could be established for as much of the disarmament process as possible. It would clearly be necessary to ensure that warhead components could not be removed and secreted away at any time during the dismantlement process. To enable this, warhead containers would need to be sealed with devices that could reliably detect any unauthorised attempt to open them.[14]

Although there are undoubtedly sensitivities associated with international inspectors being permitted into nuclear-weapons storage and deployment sites, the problems do not seem insurmountable. As part of the verification arrangements for START, for instance, inspectors are allowed to count the re-entry vehicles in the nose cone of a ballistic missile, which are covered in such a way that inspectors cannot learn sensitive design details. Indeed, in general, managed-access techniques are relatively well understood and developed.[15] International inspectors would need only a slightly greater degree of access in order to verify the baseline declarations described above.

During verification, inspectors would not be permitted to inspect the warheads themselves, only their containers. It would therefore be necessary to provide evidence that real warheads were inside the containers. Some confidence might be built by establishing a robust chain of custody for the warheads, starting from the place where they were stored or deployed. In addition, it would probably also be necessary to authenticate the warheads by measuring their properties in a way that did not reveal classified design details. This step, potentially the weakest link in the dismantlement process, is discussed further below.

Having been authenticated, warheads would then be dismantled away from international inspectors.[16] The perimeter and portals of dismantlement facilities (or any other facility in which it was permitted to open the containers) would need to be continually monitored to detect unauthorised removals.[17] The effort required in the verification process would be substantially reduced to the extent that automatic, rather than human, monitoring were feasible. Dismantlement facilities would also need to be periodically 'swept' by inspectors to ensure that no warhead components had been retained. The recovered fissile material would be converted into forms from which sensitive information (such as shape, mass and fabrication technique) could not be inferred, and placed under standard international safeguards. The non-nuclear components of warheads would be destroyed. Depending on the sensitivity of the component in question, it might be possible for this to be done in the presence of inspectors. High explosive, for instance, burns in a very characteristic way, and there would be no reason why inspectors could not witness its destruction, so long as they did not learn sensitive details about its shape.

Extensive efforts have been made elsewhere to elaborate this model in much greater depth than can be presented here and, on balance, it seems that verification of the dismantling of declared warheads is within the realms of possibility. This is not to say that all problems have been solved. For instance, given the importance of containment and the establishment of reliable chains of custody during the dismantlement process, there are real questions about whether current tags and seals are up to the job.[18] Nonetheless, such problems should not be insurmountable, given sufficient political will and funding. The one possible exception to this generally optimistic conclusion is the problem of authenticating warheads. Although current approaches may ultimately prove successful, there are reasons, outlined immediately below, to believe that this may become a sticking point.

ii. Are information barriers the solution to the authentication problem?

Russia and the US have already given considerable thought to the problem of how to authenticate warheads. Research has centred on the concept of information barriers.[19] In this approach, inspectors would measure the radioactive emissions of a warhead in a container using standard detectors. But because inspectors are not permitted to view the output of the scanner directly, as this might disclose sensitive design details, an 'information barrier' would be used to filter the output of the detector and remove sensitive information. In principle, the filtered output could be nothing more than a green or red light indicating whether or not a genuine warhead was present inside the container.

The principal difficulty of information-barrier technology is the problem of arriving at a formula for determining whether or not the object inside the box is a warhead. One approach, known as attribute verification, involves essentially defining a warhead as an object that possesses a certain set of characteristics. For instance, any object that contained a certain minimum mass of plutonium of a particular range of isotopic compositions could be deemed to be a warhead. This was the method favoured by the Trilateral Initiative, a joint project between Russia, the US and the IAEA to permit the verification of plutonium derived from weapons.

Although this method holds considerable promise, it leaves a number of questions unanswered, not least where the cut-off point should be. How much plutonium or uranium must an object contain before it is deemed to be a warhead? Because the quantity of fissile material in a warhead is classified, all an inspected party can do is declare that a given warhead contains at least, say, 4kg of uranium, and hope that other parties accept its figures. But would states be willing to take such declarations on trust? This problem is perhaps most acute for non-nuclear-weapons states, who ought not to possess detailed information about the design of nuclear weapons. How could they assess, without undertaking proscribed research, whether such claims were reasonable? Would Saudi Arabia or Syria, for example, be likely to accept a verification system based on Israeli claims about the designs of its nuclear weapons?

Even if acceptable attributes could somehow be chosen, attribute verification cannot provide assurance that none of the fissile material from a nuclear weapon has been diverted. It is frequently overlooked that authenticating a warhead using the attribute method is not equivalent to verifying that no fissile material has been removed from a warhead.[20] This deficiency in attribute verification may not matter much in today's world, where nuclear-armed states have large stockpiles of fissile material, and so little incentive for clandestine diversion, but it could become significant as zero levels were approached.

This discussion should not be taken to imply that authenticating warheads is impossible. To some extent its feasibility depends on a political judgement about the degree of confidence required from the verification process. At a technical level, it may well be possible to overcome the problems highlighted here. Even if attribute verification could not be made to work, it is possible that an alternative (or potentially complementary) technology, template verification, could. Template verification involves comparing the radioactive spectrum of the object under verification to a 'template' spectrum, and determining whether the object is a warhead on the basis of how similar its spectrum is to the template. This technology suffers from its own set of problems, not least regarding how such a template could be created, and it is not currently the leading candidate.[21] But what this discussion does demonstrate is that more work is required to solve the problem of verifying the dismantling of declared warheads, and that technologies appropriate for US–Russian bilateral agreements in today's world may not be suitable for wider use in a world moving towards zero nuclear armouries. Moreover, nuclear-weapons states need to build confidence in authentication technology among non-nuclear-weapons states. To this end, as well as continuing to research information-barrier technology by and amongst themselves, nuclear-weapons states should also co-operate in its development – so far as is possible within the constraints of Article I of the NPT – with non-nuclear-weapons states (as the UK has already begun to do with Norway).

Finally, nuclear-armed states should begin a review of their warhead classification rules and decide whether, in the context of a treaty on complete nuclear disarmament, additional information about warhead design might be released to an inspectorate. If nuclear-armed states felt able to declassify the quantity and isotopic composition of fissile material in their warheads, this would significantly simplify verification. Ultimately, nuclear-armed states would have to weigh the verification benefits against the proliferation risks of releasing such information.[22] Information would not need to be made public now, but it would facilitate the development of a verification system if there were a willingness to release it in future as part of a global move towards a nuclear-weapons-free world.

iii. Dealing with fissile material, delivery systems and infrastructure

Verification would of course also be concerned with treaty-limited items other than warheads. Warheads do, however, pose the biggest challenge and, by comparison, verifying the disposal of fissile material, the elimination of delivery systems and the shutdown or conversion of infrastructure would be relatively straightforward. Delivery vehicles, for instance, have been the subject of many arms-control negotiations. Their size makes verification relatively straightforward. Although each type of delivery system undoubtedly presents its own specific set of challenges, a wealth of experience of verifying delivery systems exists, and there appear to be no insoluble problems. The size of assembly and disassembly facilities and many other parts of a nuclear-weapons complex means that verifying their status is also unlikely to present major technical difficulties, even though currently experience of such verification is limited.[23]

A disarmament treaty would probably require states to dispose of all the fissile material from dismantled weapons. HEU can be 'denatured' through down-blending – that is, mixing it with uranium of a lower enrichment to form low-enriched uranium (LEU), from which standard reactor fuel can be fabricated. This is a straightforward process. Indeed, following a 1993 agreement, Russia down-blends around 30 tonnes of HEU per year for sale to the US. There are two long-term options for disposing of excess plutonium: 'immobilising' it by burying it along with intensely radioactive nuclear waste, thereby making it extremely difficult to extract, or burning it in a civilian power reactor as mixed-oxide (MOX) fuel to generate electricity. Immobilisation technology is unproven, and a planned US immobilisation plant is at least ten years behind schedule. Although MOX fuel has been successfully fabricated and used in Europe for several years, MOX fuel plants in the US and Russia are also at least a decade behind schedule. Moreover, the US Department of Energy estimates that it will cost around $10 billion to build and operate plutonium-disposal facilities in the US (although this must be offset against the value of the fuel thereby produced). Nevertheless, standard techniques exist for verifying the processing of fissile material. Whether such techniques are adequate is addressed in Chapter 3, where IAEA safeguards are discussed.

iv. Next steps: demonstrating proof of concept

In spite of our generally optimistic conclusions about the feasibility of verifying declared warheads, it is important to note that no state has ever actually verified the end-to-end process of dismantling and decommissioning one nuclear warhead. Various bilateral treaties have given the

US and Russia experience of verifying parts of the nuclear-disarmament process.[24] But no part of the warhead-dismantlement process has ever been verified, although much of the relevant technology has been investigated (most notably in the Trilateral Initiative).

The US and Russia could take a significant step that could earn them credit at the 2010 NPT Review Conference by agreeing and adopting a prototype end-to-end verification scheme for the dismantling and decommissioning of one or more warheads.[25] Verification should start with the removal of the warhead from its delivery system and end with the placing of its fissile material under international safeguards. By demonstrating verifiable disarmament in the form that most people envisage when they think of eliminating nuclear arsenals, the US and Russia would identify challenges, show goodwill and perhaps begin a process of acculturating key institutions to the vision of a world without nuclear weapons. The conference of weapons laboratories from the NPT nuclear-weapons states proposed by the UK would be an important complementary initiative, offering the P5 a forum in which to explore further the scope for cooperation on verification technologies and procedures.

Assessing completeness: worrying about what is not declared

The preceding discussion surveyed the technology available for verifying the dismantling and disposal of declared nuclear warheads and other treaty-limited items. But the question arises of why states would go to the trouble of trying to defeat a verification system when they could simply fail to declare hidden warheads. Retaining warheads clandestinely would be easier and cheaper, and there would be much less risk of being caught. Warheads are small and easily moveable. Although radioactive, they can easily be shielded, and there is no realistic hope that radiation detectors could find them at distances of more than a few metres. The problem is not limited to warheads; a state capable of manufacturing fissile material would have no difficulties in keeping an illicit stockpile secret.

The detection of clandestine stocks of warheads, warhead sub-assemblies and fissile material presents a much bigger challenge to disarmament than does the authentication of declared warheads. Yet the latter, easier question has attracted far more attention. For a prohibition on nuclear weapons to be embraced, nuclear-armed states would need to be convinced that the risks associated with not disarming outweighed the risk of major failures in the verification and enforcement regime. They would be much more likely to reach this conclusion if they were confident that there was a reasonable chance of clandestine stockpiles of warheads and fissile material being detected. In this section we address what can be done. There is no single solution, but a number of overlapping techniques may be applied, ranging from verifying past production of fissile material to gathering intelligence on current activities.

i. Accounting for past production and current holdings of fissile materials

Two key functions in the disarmament process would be served by accounting for past production and current holdings of fissile material. Firstly, comparing production with current holdings might enable confidence to be built that states had not clandestinely retained fissile material (whether or not in the form of warheads). Secondly, an inventory of current holdings would form the baseline for future efforts to ensure that fissile material was not diverted. Moreover, accurate accounting has an important role to play in preventing and detecting the theft of fissile material, and hence in bolstering efforts to prevent proliferation and nuclear terrorism. Most of the steps discussed below are therefore probably worth undertaking in any event, irrespective of progress towards complete disarmament. (For this reason, the marginal cost of verifying disarmament may not be especially great).

States would first be required to submit to an inspectorate comprehensive declarations of their current stocks and past fissile-material production and use. Such declarations would probably need to cover all weapons-usable fissile materials (such as uranium-233 and neptunium-237), and not only uranium-235 and plutonium. Compiling and verifying these declarations would be far from straightforward, and it would be difficult to prove their accuracy.

One particular challenge would be ensuring that declarations accurately accounted for all past production. The problem lies not so much in the possibility that a nuclear-armed state might have produced fissile material in secret facilities, though this is a possibility, as with the challenge of verifying that declared facilities have been operated as stated, sometimes over the course of many years.[26] The difficulty is that states' own records are the principal – and sometimes only – source of evidence. Some confidence in these records could be built by checking that they were internally consistent. The greater the range of material available for cross-checking, the more confidence would be built. In some states, the range of records available will be quite large, and will include plant-operating records for all stages of the fuel cycle, financial receipts and planning, plant-maintenance and warhead-assembly and disassembly records. In other states, available sources are more limited. In Russia, for instance, the 'only comprehensive plutonium accounting scheme' is believed to consist of financial records documenting transfers of final plutonium product from the Ministry of Atomic Energy to the Ministry of Defence.[27]

Traditional forensic analysis could also be useful in verifying states' records, for example in checking that the paper on which documents are printed is the right age. Unfortunately, one side effect of the switch from paper to computer records over the past two decades is that doctoring records has become easier and less time-consuming. In addition, records stretching back over 50 years are inevitably incomplete and sometimes erroneous. If verification of past production were limited to the examination of records provided by states, it would be possible for a determined and careful violator to cheat by altering those records.

One source of independent evidence is a branch of nuclear forensics known as nuclear archaeology. Most plutonium for weapons was manufactured in graphite-moderated reactors, and the amount of plutonium produced in such reactors can be reconstructed using nuclear-archaeology techniques to analyse the trace isotopes that accumulate in graphite during reactor use.[28] But, although such techniques can reduce uncertainties, they cannot eliminate them. Moreover, forensic techniques relating to heavy-water reactors (which account for 11 of the world's 45 plutonium-production reactors) and enrichment plants (which account for the majority of past fissile-materials production) are much less accurate. In addition, many facilities in which fissile material was produced, such as a number of gaseous-diffusion facilities, have been shut down, and some have also been partially dismantled, further limiting the use of nuclear forensics.

The problems do not stop at verifying past production. Inevitable measurement errors introduce discrepancies between declarations and measured quantities of current holdings. The IAEA faces this problem today even when dealing with comparatively small quantities of fissile material.[29] Under today's safeguards standard, the agency aims to detect the diversion of a 'significant quantity' of nuclear material, defined as 'the approximate amount of nuclear material for which the possibility of manufacturing a nuclear explosive device cannot be excluded'. This quantity is currently set at 25kg for HEU and 8kg for plutonium. Given that HEU production in the US and Russia is measured in many hundreds of tonnes, verifying US and Russian HEU holdings to within a significant quantity thus defined would require an unattainable measurement error of less than 0.01%. An excellent illustration of the problem and its possible consequences in a disarmament context can be seen in efforts made by the UK and the US on a number of occasions over the past 15 years to account for their fissile

	UK		US	
	Plutonium (tonnes)	HEU (tonnes)	Plutonium (tonnes)	HEU (tonnes of U-235)[30]
Amount recorded in state's inventory	3.22	21.64	102.3	623.5
Actual holdings	3.51	21.86	99.5	620.3
Material unaccounted for	-0.29	-0.22	2.8	3.2
Material unavailable for verification	>0.2	>0.6	>3.4	>10

Table 1: Results of exercises by the US and the UK to account for their plutonium and HEU production and holdings, undertaken between 1994 and 2002. Actual holdings were correct as of the following dates: 31 March 1999 (UK plutonium), 31 March 2002 (UK HEU), 30 September 1994 (US plutonium), 30 September 1996 (US HEU).

material.[31] The first row of Table 1 shows how much fissile material the two countries calculated ought to be present, according to inventories based on their records; the second row shows how much was actually measured to be present. The proportionately minor discrepancy between these sets of figures, shown in the third row of the table, is designated as 'material unaccounted for'. In the case of the US, the material unaccounted for would be enough to build around a thousand warheads. It would be a formidable challenge for the US to convince other states that none of this material had been retained in a clandestine stockpile. And the UK and US accounts were probably among the most accurate in the nuclear-armed states; the uncertainties for the Russian programme in particular are likely to be much higher.[32] A former high-ranking Chinese nuclear official reflected his nation's sensitivity to these issues when he observed in a recent conversation with one of the authors that the inevitable uncertainties in US and Russian fissile-material production inventories were greater than China's total fissile-material production. Given this, reassuring China about the possibility of major powers' evasion of a total ban on nuclear weapons would not be an easy task.[33]

There is a second, distinct challenge that would arise in the context of nuclear-disarmament verification. Much of the fissile material listed in states' declarations would not be available for verification. Substantial quantities have, for example, been used in nuclear detonations. Other material, such as that used in reactors, transformed by radioactive decay or lost in waste streams during processing, is extremely hard to verify with any accuracy. Moreover, much fissile material is held in classified form. Weapons pits, for instance, have classified shapes, masses and isotopic compositions, making it impossible for inspectors to verify the amount of material present in a pit (although, as discussed above, information about the isotopic composition and possibly mass of warheads could perhaps be declassified for inspection purposes). Similar limitations apply to naval reactor fuel. Under current rules, even material that was once in weapons but has now been converted into other forms is still sensitive, unless it has been blended in such a way as to hide its original isotopic composition. Whereas a national agency could verify all classified material, international inspectors could not (recall that information-barrier technology does not permit inspectors to measure the quantity of fissile material in a warhead).

Thus, substantial amounts of the fissile material that states have produced would, for various reasons, be unavailable for verification. Inspectors would have to take on trust the inspected state's claims about the whereabouts of this material. They would have no way of knowing that the material had not been diverted to a clandestine stockpile in violation of a disarmament agreement. This would not be a concern for national inspectors conducting an internal audit (such as the UK and US stocktakings described above), but it would concern international inspectors charged with verifying disarmament. Shown in the fourth row of Table 1 are very conservative estimates of the quantities of fissile material produced by the UK and the US that would be unavailable for verification, derived solely from estimates of material used in tests (as such material is impossible to verify).[34] In practice, because of classification rules and the material that is made extremely hard to verify by process losses, use in a reactor, decay, or transportation abroad, these quantities would probably be a great deal larger.

In short, substantial uncertainties in fissile-material inventories are unavoidable. Even with blameless intentions and honest accounting, such uncertainties would be on the order of at least a few per cent of production. Given that it is impossible to account for material to an accuracy anywhere near one nuclear weapon's worth, states would need to take a decision about how much effort and money they were prepared to expend attempting to verify past production and current holdings.

Although the problems of accounting for past production become most important in the context of abolishing nuclear weapons, they may start to be addressed before this stage is reached if the proposed Fissile Material Control Initiative (a voluntary scheme 'to increase security, transparency, and control over fissile material stocks')[35] is implemented, or if, less probably, the still-to-be-negotiated Fissile Material Cut-Off Treaty (FMCT) requires the declaration and verification of existing stocks. If either of these arrangements can be agreed upon and reasonably successfully implemented, this could build confidence in declarations of fissile-material holdings and help to pave the way towards abolition.

ii. Challenge inspections

On-site inspections are sometimes suggested as a possible solution to the problem of clandestine warheads and fissile materials. If the international body charged with verifying disarmament – or, depending on the terms of the prohibition agreement, a state party to it – had reason to suspect that a state had retained proscribed items or materials, it could demand a 'nuclear challenge' inspection to investigate further. In an extreme case, a challenge inspection might theoretically involve 'any time, anywhere' access. While challenge inspections would be likely to form an important part of any verification regime, a number of problems would need to be solved if they were to be as useful as they might at first appear.

Intrusive inspections risk compromising secrets that a state has legitimate reason to keep. These could be nuclear-related – for example, there may be commercially sensitive information, such as advanced centrifuge designs, that states and companies will want to keep secret. Classified information about conventional weapons programmes is, however, more likely to cause problems. When, for example, evidence of a possible link between Iran's nuclear programme and its military complex at Parchin, near Tehran, came to light, the IAEA's request for inspection access became highly contentious for this reason.

Curtailing the access rights of inspections can severely limit their utility and credibility, but is necessary in order for them to be acceptable to states. No state has ever voluntarily permitted 'any time, anywhere' access. South Africa came close to doing so, but only after it had dismantled its arsenal, and Iraq was forced to accept such an inspection in 1991. The most intrusive form of challenge inspection yet negotiated was that developed for the 1993 Chemical Weapons Convention (CWC). Under the convention, if a state obtains evidence that another may be secretly manufacturing chemical weapons, it may request that the Organisation for the Prohibition of Chemical Weapons conduct a challenge inspection at the suspect location. In theory, a challenge inspection could take place anywhere, including at a nuclear-weapons-production facility. However, the host state is still permitted to manage access, for example by removing 'sensitive papers from office spaces' or shrouding 'sensitive displays, stores and equipment'. Furthermore, the host state is only required to give such access as is consistent with any 'constitutional obligations it may have with regard to proprietary rights or searches and seizures' and national-security concerns.[36] Such managed access would probably impair the effectiveness of inspections to detect secret stockpiles of nuclear weapons or material.

An interesting aspect of the access problem relates to the issue of freedom of movement across international borders. The whole purpose of short-notice inspections is defeated if states have advance warning of the inspectors' arrival. However, states that issue single-entry visas for inspectors, or even simply scan passports at the point of entry, receive warning as soon as this information is processed. Iran effectively receives notice of an inspection before inspectors even leave Vienna airport, when the airline sends details of all passengers to Tehran. One – clearly expensive – solution to such problems would be to base inspectors permanently in a state. Another might be to allow inspectors complete freedom of movement across international borders, as they already have within Europe's Schengen zone, but this could be unacceptable to many states.

There are considerable political barriers to challenge inspections taking place at all. There has never been a CWC challenge inspection, despite suspicions that some of the convention's signatories may retain banned capabilities. The failure to instigate a single inspection in the 11 years that the convention has been in force seems to have increased reluctance to use them. In the nuclear context, the IAEA has a similarly powerful right to conduct so-called 'special inspections', but it has only ever requested one, in North Korea in 1993. North Korea refused access, and this failure appears to have deterred the agency's secretariat from calling any more.[37]

Finally, challenge inspections, even if agreed upon and used, would not on their own greatly increase the chances of treaty violations being detected. To be able to detect undeclared warheads or fissile material, inspectors would first need to have some idea of where to look. However, dependable evidence that proscribed items were stored in a particular undeclared location would be exceptionally hard to come by, as warheads and their components can be moved and hidden very easily. For challenge inspections to be effective, they must be backed by other instruments, such as intelligence, that have some chance of finding initial evidence of a violation.

Notwithstanding these limitations, it is difficult to envisage a disarmament agreement without challenge inspections, since the inspectorate would need some procedure for investigating allegations of the possession of clandestine warheads or fissile material. The utility of challenge inspections might be significantly increased if the body overseeing inspections and enforcement was entitled to presume guilt when a state refused to accept one.

There is much that states can do today to start ascertaining whether the problems outlined above are soluble, such as investigating whether it is possible to devise a protocol for challenge inspections that would enable the protection of legitimate secrets while still giving inspectors the access needed to detect treaty violations. Such explorations would demonstrate states' goodwill in taking seriously the obligation to negotiate towards complete nuclear disarmament.

iii. What role for intelligence?

The image of a clandestine stockpile consisting of a few warheads gathering dust in a basement is a potentially misleading one. Physicist Richard Garwin has pointed out that, given the importance of keeping nuclear weapons safe and secure, there is likely to be activity associated with any clandestine warhead stockpile:

> If a state does intend to divert its warheads ... it would have to both keep records and inform a limited number of individuals about the purpose of its covert store of nuclear weapons. Otherwise, these weapons would be of little use and of considerable hazard to its purpose. The state would also need to provide security, surveillance and, very likely, appropriate maintenance for the covert warheads, as well as the means to bring them out and mate them with delivery vehicles.[38]

Though limited, this activity would present opportunities for detection by national governments using intelligence capabilities (particularly human and signals intelligence) that are not at the disposal of international bodies such as the IAEA. The use of national intelligence by international verification bodies is controversial, not least because it risks compromising the international organisation's independence. Key questions are, therefore, whether intelligence should be formally integrated into the verification process, and whether states would be willing to share intelligence information.

There are real political advantages in an international verification body being seen as independent, objective and unconnected to national governments. On the other hand, it is hard to imagine how a ban on nuclear weapons would be verifiable without leveraging the world's intelligence capabilities. Article VIII.A of the IAEA's statute permits the agency to receive information from member states, and intelligence has played an important role in some IAEA operations. The US, for instance, provided satellite imagery to the agency when it was attempting to verify

North Korea's initial declaration in 1992 and 1993.[39] This evidence helped the IAEA to plan its inspections, and ultimately to prove North Korea's non-compliance with NPT obligations. Nonetheless, intelligence is not generally a key source of information for the IAEA. The extent to which intelligence should be used by the international body charged with verifying disarmament is an issue that states should discuss.

National intelligence agencies are generally reluctant to share information with each other or with the IAEA. The UK and US, for instance, became aware of Libya's clandestine centrifuge programme in 2000 through their intelligence on the A.Q. Khan network,[40] but the IAEA only learnt about it in 2003. Indeed, there was apparently so little communication between the UK, the US and the IAEA over Libya that the IAEA was reportedly informed about Gadhafi's decision to abandon Libya's WMD programme by television news. Irrespective of the rights and wrongs of the decisions not to share intelligence in this case, a lack of willingness to share intelligence in a nuclear-weapons-free world would seem to be a lost opportunity for much-needed verification. The inspectorate would be the obvious coordinator for intelligence information. By comparing states' intelligence reports with each other and with information from its own inspectors, states' declarations and open-source literature, the inspectorate would be able to draw a more complete picture than could any individual state's intelligence service.

Greater willingness on the part of states to share intelligence with international organisations will come about only with increased trust that international civil servants will not disclose such information to their states of origin or other actors. At the same time, the international organisation tasked with verifying disarmament would need to have confidence that intelligence provided by a state was genuine, and not an attempt to frame an enemy. The required levels of trust cannot be built quickly, but there are numerous opportunities for national governments and international bodies to cooperate more closely and test the extent to which intelligence can be usefully employed in international verification.

In their efforts to detect and prevent terrorism, the US, the European Union and others are developing and deploying monitoring systems and other intelligence-gathering capabilities that could be used to strengthen verification of a nuclear-weapons ban. Though it was not initially conceived for arms-control or non-proliferation purposes, port and border-crossing surveillance, including radiation detection, could turn out to be a useful contribution to verification. Similarly, the Proliferation Security Initiative is not generally considered a disarmament tool, but the international cooperation and occasional interdiction activities associated with it could offer a model for a robust verification system.

Transparency as a sign of good faith?

Lessons from South Africa

Though each is far from infallible, the verification techniques described above could, if used in combination with each other, certainly help to build confidence that states had not clandestinely retained prohibited items and materials. However, central to the challenge of verification is the problem of 'proving a negative', of verifying the absence of something. The IAEA faces this problem when it tries to draw, in safeguards terminology, a 'broader conclusion' from its investigations about 'the absence of undeclared nuclear activities' in states with an Additional Protocol in force.[41] The issue is whether the absence of evidence really does constitute evidence of absence, and on what grounds it is rational to decide that it does.

One state, South Africa, did manage – in effect – to prove this negative, after it dismantled its nuclear-weapons programme in the early 1990s. It is useful to explore how it did so. Between 1990 and 1993, South Africa unilaterally dismantled the six completed nuclear weapons and an unfinished seventh that it had secretly produced. Verifying South Africa's declared fissile-material stocks was relatively straightforward; verifying its production history to confirm the absence of undeclared fissile material proved much harder. Though the quantity of HEU produced by South Africa was small (even by comparison with that of a very modest producer of HEU such as the UK), the IAEA could not be certain that all material had been accounted for. Discussing the process in 1992, then-IAEA Director General Hans Blix remarked that 'there is inherent difficulty in verifying the completeness of an original inventory in a country in which a substantial nuclear program has been going on for a long time'.[42] After extensive investigations, the IAEA could conclude nothing more definite than that 'having regard to the uncertainties normally associated with data of this nature, it is reasonable to conclude that the uranium-235 balance ... of the pilot plant is consistent with uranium feed'.[43]

Nonetheless, South Africa did succeed in convincing the IAEA and, more importantly, the world at large that it had completely dismantled its weapons programme and returned all HEU to peaceful use.[44] It did so by being highly transparent and cooperative. It briefed inspectors on the history of its programme and gave them unfettered access to all relevant facilities, records, materials and personnel. Where discrepancies arose, it cooperated fully to resolve them. Ultimately what built trust that South

Africa had not secretly retained any HEU was not the results of technical IAEA verification activities, which were not conclusive, so much as South Africa's open and transparent behaviour.[45]

Making the transparency model more broadly applicable

At first sight, it would seem a formidable task for the current nuclear-armed states to build confidence through transparency. All of them have manufactured many more nuclear weapons and produced much more fissile material than South Africa ever did. Greater transparency will not prove the absence of small clandestine stockpiles.

Criticism along these lines, however, misses the point. Transparency measures would not be expected to furnish information that would magically enable declarations to be rigorously verified. They would certainly enable further checking for internal consistency, but that would not be their primary purpose. That purpose would be to demonstrate good faith. Transparency would signal that a state had nothing to hide, and thus might make it possible for the international community to accept an imperfect verification process.

Crucially, in the South African case, the government had little incentive to cheat on its pledge of nuclear disarmament: it had just undergone a widely supported and applauded process of regime change and was keen to repudiate much that was associated with the previous regime, and its security concerns had been attenuated. Furthermore, it posed no threats to its neighbours or to the major powers. It seems likely that, had there been more scepticism about South Africa's intentions, states might have been less willing to accept that it had fully disarmed on the basis of inconclusive verification results. In the transition to a world free from nuclear weapons, where doubts about intentions might well persist, it would be a much greater challenge to make confidence-building through transparency sufficient to compensate for technical deficiencies in verification.

The value of transparency as a tool of the disarmament process would grow to the extent that there was a formalised process by which states would be required to provide detailed and comprehensive declarations of past and present activities in the form of 'nuclear histories',[46] permit visits to all relevant facilities and, most importantly, make all relevant personnel available for interviews. This would require a very high degree of openness on the part of states (although more modest measures, too, would still have value). Inspectors would need to be convinced that they were not being taken on a 'guided tour' designed to obscure activities that the state wanted to keep hidden.

Transparency was an important element of the confidence-building measures associated with the CWC, and the experience of implementing the CWC is instructive. States negotiating the CWC decided that the start date for declarations would be 1 January 1946. The start of the Second World War might be a loosely equivalent date in a nuclear context, but there would be difficulties associated with requiring extensive nuclear histories with an early start date. First, would there be any real value in declaring facilities that, by the time nuclear weapons were abolished, would be more than a century old, or long since destroyed? Some CWC inspections have taken place quite literally in the middle of fields because the facilities being inspected had long since been demolished.[47] Would similar visits in a nuclear context be worth the effort? Would transparency really be served by a visit made in 2058 to the recently closed US weapons-pit-production facility at Rocky Flats?

The scope of the declarations required by the CWC is also very broad. Article III.1.c.(i) of the CWC requires a state to declare 'any chemical-weapons production facility under its ownership or possession'. Similar phrasing could pose difficult definitional questions in a nuclear context. For instance, would states be required to declare factories that made ballistic casings for a range of weapons, including nuclear ones? If so, what should be done about factories that made the metal for the ballistic casings, or constructed more specialised components, such as altimeters?

More importantly, some nuclear-weapons states may be simply unable to provide the information required. The first generation of weapons designers is dead and, as discussed above, many early records from nuclear programmes have been lost or destroyed, if indeed they ever existed. Incomplete histories could actually be counterproductive, by giving the false impression that states had something to hide. These difficulties could be avoided by shortening and narrowing the scope of the histories, but this might then detract from their confidence-building value.

To prevent the problem of incomplete records from worsening, nuclear-armed states should establish national commissions to start compiling these histories now, even if they keep them secret for the time being. The information on fissile-material production and holdings released by the US and UK discussed above is a significant precedent – and it is to those states' credit that this information was made public. States should make concerted efforts to retain key documents and records in a form that permits forensic analysis to confirm that they are genuine (which might mean, for instance, keeping paper records). They should also conduct and record interviews with key scientists. Seminars with several witnesses might be even more useful, as participants could jog one another's memories. The value of all this would be substantially enhanced if states were able to agree among themselves standards for the compilation of nuclear histories and the preservation of data.

Interviews with key personnel would be valuable in clarifying and verifying nuclear histories. States that permitted the inspectorate to interview key figures in each of their nuclear-weapons and fissile-material-production programmes would send a strong message that they had nothing to hide. Such interviews could not be hostile examinations; states would not willingly subject their nuclear scientists and engineers, many of whom would possess extensive knowledge of highly classified programmes, to the sorts of interrogation faced by defeated parties in war. Rather, responsible experts working for an international inspectorate would cull oral histories from knowledgeable figures in each nuclear-weapons programme to check individual accounts against each other and the written record.

The IAEA recognises the great value of interviewing key personnel in nuclear programmes for resolving questions of compliance and verifying disarmament, a value that was demonstrated in Iraq in the 1990s. However, recent experience does not bode well for the practice. In negotiations on the CTBT (which still has not entered into force), the US, Russia, China and others refused to include in the treaty explicit authorisation of the use of interviews in the verification process.[48] Iran has not acceded to all IAEA requests to interview leaders of its nuclear programme, despite Security Council resolutions ordering its full cooperation and transparency.[49] Such interviews as have been granted have taken place under intimidating conditions controlled by the Iranian state. Most states with nuclear programmes of any kind are wary of having outsiders elicit information from their nuclear scientists and engineers. This culture of secrecy would need to be attenuated for the elimination of nuclear weapons to become possible.

Another issue that would need to be considered in relation to any transparency regime is that of states that had nuclear-weapons programmes at some point, but did not go on to develop nuclear weapons. Would they also be required to submit nuclear histories? Openness about programmes that are widely known about (such as those in Argentina, Australia, Brazil, Romania and Sweden) might build confidence in the intentions of those states and encourage more honest and detailed declarations from the nuclear-armed states. On the other hand, it is not clear what would be the effect of revealing programmes that were less widely known about. Such revelations could be counterproductive, increasing tensions between states and perhaps also creating discord within them (many Canadians, for instance, might be dismayed to learn that their country once had a nuclear-weapons programme).

A fundamental question about confidence-building through transparency remains whether conclusions drawn from this kind of verification would be actionable. Transparency (or the lack of it) is very influential with inspectors visiting sites, negotiating with officials and interviewing scientists. Whether these inspectors can then convince the international community of their conclusions without hard supporting evidence is another matter. For instance, as with South Africa, it would probably be impossible for inspectors to prove that a disarming Israel had declared all its plutonium. Would inspectors be able to convince Arab states, Iran and Pakistan that Israel had no clandestine stockpile on the basis that they 'felt' that Israel was not trying to hide anything? Conversely, let us imagine that inspectors came to believe that the US was trying to hide something, even though measurements of its fissile-material stockpile showed no discrepancies with the record beyond the normal margin of error. Would the international community be willing to risk derailing the entire disarmament process by attempting to force the US to cooperate with further measures, even though the inspectors' view was strictly no more than a strong suspicion? After all, the IAEA board of governors and the UN Security Council were extremely reluctant to take action against Iran even after the IAEA had provided incontrovertible evidence that Iran had breached its safeguards agreement.

Civil-society monitoring

It is often argued that technical means of verification alone would not provide sufficient assurance to enable the prohibition of nuclear weapons. Accordingly, another possible supplement to technical verification has been suggested, in addition to transparency measures: 'societal verification', or civil-society monitoring.[50] The idea behind civil-society monitoring is that the responsibility for detecting a treaty violation should rest not just with designated inspectors but with society at large. The case for making use of such monitoring would probably grow if a renaissance of the nuclear industry increased the overall amounts of verification required by bringing capabilities and expertise to new states.

Typical proposals suggest that a nuclear-disarmament treaty should require states to enact national laws making it the right – and indeed the duty – of every citizen to report any evidence of a treaty violation to an international body. Governments would be required to educate their populations about this duty. Under a global prohibition, directors and chief executive officers in nuclear-related industries could be required annu-ally to sign legal documents certifying that no production of illicit nuclear equipment or material had occurred in their enterprise.[51] Employees could be required to sign annual agreements to reveal any illicit nuclear activity of which they became aware or face prosecution, on the basis that this obli-gation would override normal corporate secrecy commitments. Parallel laws forbidding enterprises or the state from penalising or obstructing whistle-blowers or from taking retaliatory action against their families would testify to a state's commitment to adhering to a nuclear-weapons ban, as would laws granting asylum to whistle-blowers and their fami-lies from other states if needed. A further, more controversial, suggestion is that substantial monetary rewards, funded internationally, should be made available in return for information leading to the detection of viola-tions of a nuclear-weapons ban.

Few issues prompted so diverse or vigorous a range of responses from those who reviewed drafts of this paper as did civil-society monitoring. Debate centred on two key questions. Could it work? And would it be acceptable?

For civil-society monitoring to be feasible, there would need to be potential whistle-blowers and a realistic way for them to inform. Sceptics argue that in an autocratic state which demanded a high degree of loyalty from its citizens, none of the few who knew about a clandestine nuclear-weapons programme would be willing to come forward, and that the government would go to great lengths to silence any who did. The Soviet Union's success in hiding for a long time a huge biological-weapons programme that it continued in contravention of the 1972 Biological and Toxin Weapons Convention has been cited as an example of the failure of whistle-blowing. The sceptical view is that civil-society monitoring requires a free press to provide a platform for whistle-blowers and, even more importantly, to highlight state attempts to silence them, and there-fore would only really be viable in a democracy.

Advocates of civil-society monitoring argue that it is feasible in non-democratic societies because only one informer is needed. No state can command the absolute loyalty of every one of its citizens, especially in the face of the strong global norm that would come about as a result of the abolition of nuclear weapons. Moreover, with modern technology such as encrypted websites that could keep a whistle-blower's message and location secret,[52] whistle-blowing could be feasible in any country with internet access. Proponents point out that leaks from authoritarian societies are hardly unknown, especially if one includes individuals who have approached foreign intelligence services. The defection of Saddam Hussein's son-in-law Hussein Kamal from Iraq in 1995, which marked the turning-point for UN Special Commission and IAEA verification efforts, is a high-profile example. It can also be argued that the post-1972 Soviet biological-weapons programme in fact demonstrated the success of civil-society monitoring because it was eventually disclosed by an inside informant.

The question of the acceptability of societal monitoring is even more controversial than that of its efficacy. Making use of civil-society monitoring would require states to enact laws expressly intended to rank above normal national loyalty. Clearly, the issue would pose hard questions to all states, not only nuclear-armed ones, about how far they were willing to go to enable complete disarmament.

Costs: how much and who should pay?

As with almost all arms-control agreements, expense would be a major issue in negotiations about nuclear disarmament, with states trying to keep costs as low as possible. Discussions of cost centre on two important questions: 'how much?' and 'who will pay?'.

A detailed cost estimate for nuclear disarmament is beyond the scope of this paper. It is, however, an important issue, and governments and non-governmental analysts should attempt to develop estimates to help inform the debate. Various general observations can nevertheless be made. First, costs fall into two categories: the cost of verifying the transition to zero, and the ongoing cost of preventing rearmament (the safeguards needed to prevent rearmament are discussed in Chapter 3).

The cost of verifying the transition to zero, though non-recurring, would probably be substantial: verification technology would need to be developed, inspectors trained and employed, existing assembly/disassembly facilities converted to permit verification (or new ones built), perimeter monitoring installed, oral histories conducted and analysed – the list goes on. Unfortunately, the cost of verification also usually proves to be much greater than initially forecast. For instance, an early unreleased UK study suggested that the installation of the verification system for the CTBT would cost around $80 million.[53] The bill for the International Monitoring System for the CTBT (not yet complete) now appears likely to be on the order of $1 billion.[54]

The projected expense of verifying an FMCT could give some idea of the cost of the safeguards needed to prevent rearmament. The IAEA has estimated the annual verification costs of an FMCT at between 50 and 150 million euros.[55] These should, however, be regarded as lower limits, since verification in a nuclear-weapons-free world would probably need to be much more rigorous than it would for an FMCT.

But expense could also prove to be a driver of disarmament, as it was during the Cold War. A proper analysis of the cost of abolition must take into account the savings made by reducing and ultimately scrapping nuclear arsenals and their associated infrastructure. (The analysis would also need to determine whether these savings would be immediate, or realised only after the initial outlay on verification and the destruction of weapons and related facilities). All nuclear-armed states, but the US and Russia especially, spend considerable sums on their nuclear arsenals; the US spent more than $50bn on nuclear-weapons-related activities in 2006.[56] Such figures help to put the cost of verification into perspective. On this scale, the cost of verifying a nuclear-abolition agreement is likely to be modest. That is certainly the lesson from the CTBT. As a result of its unilateral decision to suspend nuclear testing in 1992, the US launched a programme of 'stockpile stewardship' to ensure the safety and reliability of its nuclear arsenal without the use of testing. Even when the costs for new facilities related to stewardship are excluded, the US spent $3.5bn on this programme in 2006.[57] Compared to this, the estimated cost of verifying the CTBT (which helps ensure that no other state gains an advantage over the US through testing), though much higher than originally expected, is very modest.

On the question of who pays for verification, the CTBT and the CWC both offer potentially influential precedents. In negotiations on the CTBT, it was suggested that the five permanent members of the Security Council (P5) should cover the cost of verification. The P5 opposed this, arguing that, since the absence of nuclear explosions was an international public good, all states should cover the cost of the treaty. Ultimately, this argument prevailed; all CTBT verification costs are allocated on the scale used by the UN to appropriate funds, adjusted for differences in participation. This is undoubtedly the funding formula that nuclear-armed states would prefer for verifying full nuclear disarmament. But the CWC offers a contrasting, and arguably more appropriate, precedent. Under the CWC, states are required to cover the costs of destroying their own chemical munitions (though Russia has been given substantial financial aid to help it to do this). Other costs, in particular those of ongoing verification, are met by all participating states, similarly on the basis of a variant on the UN formula. This system could be applied to nuclear disarmament as a compromise arrangement.

CHAPTER THREE

Managing the Nuclear Industry in a World without Nuclear Weapons

Keeping the world safe in the nuclear-energy renaissance

Calls for nuclear disarmament are intensifying just as nuclear energy is expected to expand greatly worldwide. Much more tension exists between the two objectives of nuclear disarmament and the expansion of nuclear energy than has been publicly discussed.

Shortly after the Second World War, the US, as the sole possessor of nuclear weapons, sought international agreement on a plan to control nuclear energy. The Baruch Plan and its more enlightened predecessor, the Acheson–Lilienthal Plan, were attempts to head off a nuclear-arms race by designing a framework for the international control of all nuclear activities that would prevent the production of nuclear weapons and would thereby enable the US securely to eliminate its fledgling arsenal. Since the failure of the Baruch Plan, however, the challenges of nuclear disarmament have not been addressed alongside those of managing an expansion in nuclear energy. The total elimination of nuclear arsenals almost disappeared from the international agenda until after the Cold War.[1] It briefly resurfaced with Mikhail Gorbachev's 1986 call for nuclear abolition, the Reykjavik summit in October that year and Rajiv Gandhi's 1988 speech to the UN on nuclear disarmament. But the accident at Chernobyl in April 1986 had put an end to any hopes of a significant expansion in a nuclear industry that had been in grave difficulty for some years. The NPT Extension Conference of 1995 and the Review Conference of 2000 put disarmament back on the agenda, albeit tentatively, but at that time the nuclear industry was still in the doldrums.

The potential global expansion of nuclear energy over the next decades carries proliferation risks if there are not new and reliably enforced rules for managing it and keeping it secure. But key non-nuclear-weapons states are already expressing deep reluctance to consider any new rules if the nuclear-weapons states do not undertake a yet-to-be-defined plan for nuclear disarmament.[2] At the same time, the nuclear-armed states will not agree to eliminate their nuclear arsenals if they are not confident that proliferation will be prevented through the enforcement of stronger non-proliferation rules.

This circular problem between the nuclear haves and have-nots is exacerbated by a further inequality – between those states that possess enrichment or reprocessing capabilities and those that do not. If there is to be a significant expansion of nuclear energy, global capacity to manufacture nuclear fuel will need to be increased. With demand for nuclear fuel projected to rise dramatically, several states, including Argentina, Brazil, Canada, Iran and South Africa, have either expressed an interest in developing enrichment programmes or have already begun such programmes. Many international leaders recognise that the spread of fuel-cycle facilities to non-nuclear-weapons states poses a proliferation risk.[3] States that possess such facilities for civilian purposes could use them, or associated know-how, to produce fuel for weapons. Yet the states that are either hoping to develop or are developing enrichment programmes oppose (more or less strenuously) rules to prevent the spread of dual-use fuel-cycle capabilities, partly because this would further entrench the existing inequality between fuel-cycle suppliers and recipients. If more non-nuclear-weapons states, such as those mentioned above, develop enrichment capabilities before any new rules are enacted, resistance to such rules will only intensify, especially in the Middle East and elsewhere in Asia.

Proposals to resolve this central dilemma are currently being developed. The World Nuclear Association, the IAEA and the Nuclear Threat Initiative,[4] along with a number of states, have proposed various mechanisms for assuring fuel supply in the hope that states will choose to eschew new national facilities for enriching uranium and separating plutonium.[5] In some of the proposals, fuel would only be supplied on condition that the state forgoes national fuel-cycle capabilities. A number of states would like to see an outright global ban on the spread of fuel-cycle facilities to states that do not already possess them, even if many would not say so publicly. However, because a number of key non-nuclear-weapons states, including Brazil, Egypt, Iran and South Africa, firmly reject the idea of binding rules, voluntary restraint appears to be the most that is politically feasible in the near term. But voluntary agreements whereby states agree on an ad hoc basis to forgo fuel production in return for international nuclear cooperation do not offer robust confidence that proliferation will be avoided in the long run. If states that aspire to developing major new civilian nuclear programmes will not accept binding rules to forgo enrichment and reprocessing, are there other measures that they would endorse to improve confidence that nuclear proliferation will not occur, given that current safeguards may be inadequate in a nuclear-disarming world?

In a sense, current nuclear suppliers – many of whom live under nuclear-deterrent umbrellas – and aspiring buyers and sellers are talking past each other. The former are looking for strong bulwarks against future proliferation, while the latter want to keep their options open – most wish to defend their 'nuclear rights', and perhaps to hedge against future insecurity. What has been absent is direct bargaining in which suppliers and buyers clearly articulate their interests and the trade-offs they are prepared to negotiate. Developing-country non-nuclear-weapons states have tended not to engage in creative give-and-take in addressing the global fuel-cycle challenge. This may reflect the natural tendency of the weaker party to a negotiation to wait to hear what the stronger has to offer, or it may be a consequence of a comparative lack of nuclear expertise. Whatever the cause, the reticence of future nuclear buyers leaves many questions unanswered about the future of global nuclear energy and the evolution of the non-proliferation regime. If the web of issues around nuclear energy and non-proliferation is not disentangled, it is likely that it will not be possible to reach the latter stages of nuclear disarmament, though this need not preclude many earlier steps in this direction.

Another major potential tension between the growth of nuclear energy and the elimination of nuclear arsenals centres on global shortages in capacity to produce nuclear-reactor components. For the next decade, the world's nuclear industry can probably build no more than ten reactors per year.[6] Though few – if any – of the countries that do not currently have power reactors and have expressed an interest in acquiring them are likely to have the required physical and regulatory infrastructure for handling safety, security and liability issues for the next ten to 15 years, the long lead times needed for nuclear-plant projects mean that contracts have to be drawn up many years in advance of construction, and current suppliers will enjoy a seller's market for the foreseeable future. They will prioritise buyers that already have superior nuclear expertise and related physical and social infrastructure, and which present the least risk of disruption from political turmoil or disputes about liability or payment. These buyers will tend to be in China, the US, South Korea, Europe and possibly India. For both commercial and technical reasons, established vendors will be less interested in non-nuclear-weapons states in the developing world, especially the less politically stable ones. If developing countries seeking nuclear cooperation are thereby rebuffed, and feel that their right under Article IV of the NPT to assistance in developing nuclear technology for peaceful purposes is being disregarded, they could become still further alienated from the non-proliferation regime. Key non-nuclear-weapons states might then become even less supportive than they are today of rules for managing nuclear industry, including the fuel cycle. This could, in turn, make nuclear-armed states less willing to disarm.

While it is too early to know whether supply constraints will prompt a backlash against efforts to strengthen the non-proliferation regime, representatives of states that are able to supply nuclear technology and expertise and those of states newly aspiring to develop nuclear industries should address these issues candidly. The IAEA is now constructively engaging relevant parties on these matters. These discussions could be broadened to include civil society in developing countries and leading commercial vendors.

Along with the shortfall in the global capacity to manufacture reactors, there is also a skills shortage. Even without a nuclear renaissance, finding enough inspectors to implement all the verification measures necessary to facilitate disarmament (including those discussed in the previous chapter) would be a stiff challenge. If the inspectorate has to compete with an expanding nuclear industry for personnel, the problem will be exacerbated. Clearly, if a nuclear-weapons-free-world is to be achieved alongside a global expansion of nuclear energy, considerable investment in training will be required.

Today, nuclear-weapons states and their allies are willing to tolerate weaknesses in safeguards partly because of their possession of nuclear weapons, which, they feel, protects them from some of the potential consequences of proliferation. Whether or not a rational cost–benefit analysis would show that safeguards should be strengthened in today's world, they would almost certainly need to be improved significantly if complete nuclear disarmament were to be taken seriously. This is true regardless of whether attempts to prevent the spread of fuel-cycle technology are successful.

The challenge may be complicated in the future by technological developments that could make it harder to safeguard civilian nuclear activities.

Experience in Libya and Iran (which is only now coming close to mastering centrifuge technology, over 20 years after the initiation of its enrichment programme) seems to show that the difficulty of getting centrifuge technology to work has been an important barrier against unsafeguarded fissile-material production.[7] Iraq suffered similar, if less acute, difficulties.[8] This barrier may be gradually eroded as more states acquire advanced industrial bases. It is also possible that other enrichment technologies that can be concealed more easily than the gas centrifuge will come into play over the long term. Laser enrichment, if it could be made to work on a commercial scale, would be of particular concern.[9]

There needs to be more research and debate on how the expansion of nuclear energy can be made compatible with progress toward eliminating all nuclear arsenals. It needs to involve experts beyond the nuclear industry and nuclear-weapons establishments. Non-nuclear-weapons states must be brought more fully into the process, with an understanding that emphasis should be on the practical issues at hand, rather than the issue of broader global inequities, which is better addressed in other forums. If governments lag in sponsoring such interactions, non-governmental actors should fill the gap. As a contribution to this debate, we now summarise options for strengthening control of the nuclear industry. These range from incremental improvements to existing safeguards to the radical option of eliminating the most proliferation-sensitive activities.

The evolutionary approach: improving IAEA safeguards

Against the background of the anticipated nuclear-energy renaissance, there has been much discussion of the limitations of IAEA safeguards.[10] Although it is the IAEA's ability to detect the diversion of nuclear material from declared civilian facilities that has been most questioned in the context of non-nuclear-weapons states with nuclear-power programmes, the harder task is in fact detecting undeclared nuclear facilities, especially small gas-centrifuge enrichment plants.

Many incremental improvements could be made to IAEA safeguards. One relatively inexpensive option would be to move the starting point of material accountancy further up the production chain to place all yellow-cake (refined uranium ore) under safeguards.[11] Another improvement, which would be particularly important in the context of disarmament, would be the extension of safeguards to cover other fissile materials, apart from uranium and plutonium, from which nuclear weapons could be manufactured, in particular the neptunium-237 isotope. Another option would be to increase the frequency of inspections so that diversions would be detected more rapidly; the IAEA has, however, been altering its practice in the opposite direction in the past few years.[12] A much more expensive option, deemed highly desirable by some, would be to redesign the whole safeguards system so as to be capable of detecting diversions of much smaller quantities of nuclear material.

An analysis of the politics of the verification process demonstrates that even if the political will and financing were available to implement all these changes and many more on the shopping list, it is doubtful whether safeguards, in the traditional sense, could ever be sufficient to build the confidence necessary for the abolition of nuclear weapons.

Verification is not an end in itself. It has various purposes. Among them are to deter cheating by raising the risk of detection and to trigger enforcement actions capable of bringing a state back into compliance with an international agreement it has violated. To these ends, an effective system of safeguards would fulfil three criteria. It would:

- have a high probability of detecting a violation;
- be capable of providing timely warning of a violation; and
- be able to provide convincing evidence of a violation.

It is the second and third criteria that we focus on here (although the first issue is also an important one for states to discuss; in particular, in the context of disarmament, how high is high enough?).

Currently, the IAEA aims to detect a diversion of nuclear material in about the same time as it would take a state to convert that material into a nuclear weapon.[13] The agency assesses this period to be a month for plutonium and HEU, and a year for LEU (though these figures may well be significant overestimates). Enforcement, however, has typically taken much longer than detection. The limiting factor in rectifying non-compliance is not the timeliness of the warning from the IAEA, but the time taken for enforcement action to be agreed on and to work. For instance, the warning that the international community received in August 2002 of Iran's clandestine uranium-enrichment programme was timely. However, it was almost four and a half years before the Security Council passed its first sanctions resolution in December 2006, and by July 2008, Iran had still not complied with that or two further sanctions resolutions. Changing the safeguards system so that the IAEA could detect non-compliance earlier – by, say, increasing the frequency of inspections – would do little to solve this essentially political problem.

If zero nuclear weapons were the agreed universal standard, the Security Council would probably be willing to act more rapidly in the event of a very serious violation (such as, for instance, the actual diversion of nuclear material, as opposed to the maintenance of an extensive clandestine centrifuge effort). But even if the Security Council could agree upon enforcement action in a matter of days, in such a serious case, it might already be too late to prevent the violator from manufacturing a nuclear weapon.[14] However fast the IAEA can be made to operate, complete disarmament may remain elusive as long as safeguards are designed to do nothing more than detect a violation.

A related problem arises with the third of these criteria, that of providing convincing evidence. Recent experience shows that states may view it in their interest to question the judgement of the IAEA and not immediately accept its conclusions. When Iran's clandestine nuclear programme was discovered, Russia, China and other states delayed action by insisting that the IAEA provide *proof* of Iran's intentions. The strong evidence of non-compliance presented by the IAEA was apparently not enough. (Similarly, when the IAEA discovered that South Korea had performed undeclared reprocessing and enrichment experiments, the US, its close ally, lobbied other members of the agency's board of governors to ensure that it was not found in non-compliance with its safeguards agreement.)

Actually proving that a state has violated an agreement can be very difficult and often takes time, no matter how effective and well-funded safeguards are. As mentioned above, the difficulty is probably most acute in the case of clandestine facilities. Although the Additional Protocol significantly enhances the IAEA's prospects of collecting information suggestive of undeclared nuclear activity, it may be impossible for the IAEA to prove that a clandestine facility exists unless it can inspect the suspect site (this is particularly true in the case of small clandestine enrichment plants). In practice, of course, a state with a clandestine facility would in all probability simply refuse the IAEA access. Recent experience suggests that the Security Council might not back an IAEA request for access without first requiring stronger evidence than the IAEA could provide without an inspection. Again, we have a circular problem, which is more political than it is technical. Enhanced IAEA safeguards are unlikely to inspire enough confidence to make a nuclear-weapons-free world possible unless the international community is willing to accept a considerably lower standard for assessing evidence, such as a balance of probabilities rather than proof beyond reasonable doubt.

The problem might be alleviated by closer cooperation between the IAEA and national intelligence agencies. With the possible exception of the Manhattan Project in the US, there appear to have been no instances of a state managing to build and operate a secret fuel-cycle facility of any significance without at least arousing the strong suspicions of a state with advanced intelligence assets. Whether it was Israel in the 1960s, Pakistan in the 1970s and 1980s, North Korea in the 1990s, Iran in more recent years or Syria in 2007, key states have always detected clandestine fissile-material production before weapons were produced. That not all such detections resulted in actions which prevented proliferation is due at least in part to the difficulties of using national intelligence to inform international verification activities.

Another possibility is for the IAEA to be tasked with looking for evidence of weaponisation. Currently, the IAEA's authority and ability to verify that military research and development is not connected to nuclear weapons is very limited, especially where no nuclear material is involved.[15] Tasking the IAEA with detecting weaponisation activities might be an important additional protection in a nuclear-weapons-free world (and indeed in today's world), increasing both the probability of detecting a violation and the warning time provided. However, it would be expensive, difficult and potentially controversial. For instance, there is no universal agreement on what – apart from the discovery of certain nuclear-weapon components or a few particular activities – would constitute evidence of a nuclear-weapons programme.

The radical approach: multinational or international ownership of fuel-cycle facilities

One alternative to traditional safeguards on nuclear facilities owned by states is for the fuel cycle to be 'multinationalised' (where facilities are owned and operated by a coalition of states) or even internationalised (with ownership and operation in the hands of an international body, as envisaged by the Acheson–Lilienthal Plan). Some commentators have gone so far as to argue that it would be impossible to move to a nuclear-weapons-free world without first placing all enrichment and reprocessing facilities, and possibly all nuclear materials as well, under multinational or international ownership or control (in addition to IAEA safeguards).[16] Would India be willing to dismantle its last nuclear warhead if the Khan Research Laboratories in Pakistan were still enriching uranium under exclusive Pakistani control, albeit under the watchful eye of IAEA inspectors? Even if India did prove willing, it would almost certainly be on the condition that India itself could continue plutonium production under exclusively Indian control, in which case the existence of nationally controlled fuel-cycle capabilities could test the stability of Indo-Pakistani relations. In another part of the world, if Japan and China continued national fuel-cycle activities for peaceful purposes and under safeguards, would other Asian states seek similar national fuel-cycle capabilities? The chances of their doing so might be lessened if greater non-nuclear extended deterrence from the US were offered, but that could raise other alarms, as discussed in Chapter 1.

Moving beyond nationally owned fuel-cycle facilities could be a key step towards disarmament, and it is a concept that states should discuss seriously – though specifying and implementing the procedures to make the transition would be hugely complicated and politically challenging.[17] There is no precedent for a key facet of a major modern industry being collectively owned by a number of multinational firms, let alone being owned in its entirety by a single international organisation. At present, the idea meets firm resistance from almost every state and enterprise now producing fissile materials, especially the states with nuclear weapons. Nevertheless, two multinational enrichment organisations – the Urenco consortium and Eurodif – do already exist. As a private firm, the former in particular might offer a useful guide for further investigations.

Multinationalisation or internationalisation of the fuel cycle would not completely assuage proliferation concerns. The problem of clandestine fuel-cycle facilities would remain. While multinational or international ownership could help, by restricting or fragmenting knowledge to try to ensure that as few individual workers as possible had end-to-end knowledge of sensitive processes and that nationality groups within the workforce did not collectively have such knowledge, some workers would still learn proliferation-sensitive information. Indeed, the infamous A.Q. Khan network grew out of Urenco, insofar as Khan stole blueprints, components and valuable procurement information while employed by one of the consortium's contractors as a junior scientist. For a multinational fuel-cycle consortium to operate effectively, like any organisation, it must have senior managers with a good knowledge of the entire process. There will always be a risk that these personnel could put this expertise to prohibited uses.

Moreover, ownership would not guarantee control. Shared or international ownership might make it more embarrassing for a state to be found diverting nuclear material from a facility on its territory, and increase the penalties for its doing so, but it would not necessarily prevent such diversion.

States would need to assess the risk of a host government 'sending in the troops', physically taking control of an enrichment or reprocessing plant and using it to produce fissile material for weapons.

In theory, this problem could be minimised by locating fuel-cycle facilities on the territory of 'completely trustworthy' states. In practice, domestic pressure might make any such states reluctant to play host, especially if the facility in question were a reprocessing plant dealing with imported nuclear waste. Besides, for the sake of equity, multinational fuel-cycle facilities would probably need to be hosted by a number of states in different regions. Furthermore, perhaps most importantly, the chances of the international community agreeing on which states were 'completely trustworthy' currently appear slim.

There are many different possible models for multinational or international control of the fuel cycle. Key questions include what facilities should be included (just enrichment and reprocessing plants, or all nuclear facilities?) and precisely how these facilities should be owned and operated. States, the nuclear industry and civil society should start to consider which models might best assuage proliferation concerns, which are the most feasible politically and which make best economic sense. These investigations should help to shape the important debate about how to guarantee supply to states that lack the capability to manufacture their own nuclear fuel. It is vital that such discussions include both potential suppliers and consumers.

Non-nuclear-weapons states are unlikely to agree to new rules or arrangements for limiting access to fuel-cycle capabilities unless all states play by the same rules. Genuine commitment to and movement towards nuclear disarmament would go a long way towards satisfying the demand for equity, but might not overcome resistance to discriminatory approaches to fuel-cycle management. If nuclear-armed states, and perhaps others, do not want all states to retain the right to enrich uranium and separate plutonium on a national basis as they see fit under safeguards, the most acceptable alternative would be to move towards a standard whereby only multinational facilities were allowed everywhere, notwithstanding the difficulties involved. This issue of nuclear equity will be among the most crucial and challenging that states will face in the nuclear realm, whether or not abolition becomes a priority.

Can the most sensitive nuclear activities be compatible with a nuclear-weapons-free world?

Historically, arms-control treaties have sought to regulate, rather than ban, even the most sensitive dual-use technologies. In contemplating whether and how to achieve a world free of nuclear weapons, states must consider whether the most sensitive nuclear activities would need to be banned outright. Even a discussion about banning reprocessing is anathema to some. Nevertheless, if no acceptable form of regulation can be established for the proliferation-sensitive activities that many states which today promote disarmament are seeking to conduct, the abolition of nuclear weapons may not prove possible.

Reprocessing

Along with enrichment, reprocessing is the most proliferation-sensitive part of the fuel cycle. Historically, the failure to coordinate plutonium production with MOX fuel fabrication has led to the emergence of large plutonium stockpiles.[18] Linking plutonium production more closely to demand would help to reduce these stockpiles and promote disarmament. By itself, however, this step would be unlikely to completely assuage proliferation concerns. Current reprocessing technology produces separated plutonium, and this is the most difficult part of the fuel cycle to safeguard effectively.[19] Moreover, any state with reprocessing technology could leave the NPT and use the technology to produce fissile material for nuclear weapons. This break-out potential could be highly damaging. Japan's reprocessing programme, for example, is frequently criticised as being a way of keeping a 'bomb in the basement'. In a nuclear-weapons-free world, the suspicion of those with reprocessing capabilities – whether or not it was justified – could be destabilising.

On the other hand, plutonium is a potentially valuable energy resource. In the short term – over the next few decades, say – the world is extremely unlikely to face uranium shortages, and reprocessing may continue to be uneconomic.[20] Several decades ahead, however, if there is a significant and sustained expansion of nuclear energy, the demand for reprocessing could increase considerably, as conventional uranium resources are depleted. There is, of course, still doubt about whether the nuclear renaissance will actually take place. If it does not, a ban on reprocessing might be feasible, and widely considered to be an acceptable price to pay for a nuclear-weapons-free world. If, however, the nuclear renaissance proves to be real (and it may take decades to gauge this), a ban on reprocessing might increase reliance on fossil fuels as uranium stocks diminish, damaging efforts to curtail global warming.[21] Once more, there is a web of issues that states need to disentangle. Over the long run, will reprocessing be necessary to combat climate change? Are reprocessing and nuclear disarmament incompatible? If they are, which do states care about more?

Non-nuclear-weapons use of HEU

The break-out potential of HEU is arguably greater than that of plutonium. Whereas plutonium can only be used in a complex implosion design, HEU can be used in a simple gun-type nuclear weapon, and may therefore be more attractive to less technologically advanced proliferators. It seems reasonable to assume that the prospects for eliminating all nuclear arsenals will be significantly improved if HEU is no longer used at all (or, perhaps, if it is managed under unprecedented controls, such as limiting enrichment levels so that fuel would not be usable in weapons without further enrichment).

HEU has some uses outside nuclear-weapons programmes. Much the most significant of these is as fuel for various types of nuclear reactors, including research reactors, reactors to propel naval vessels such as submarines, aircraft carriers and (Russian) civilian icebreakers, and space reactors for powering satellites.

In theory, it should be technically possible to eliminate HEU from all types of reactors. Various initiatives to eliminate HEU from most research reactors are currently under way.[22] Although some important technical challenges remain, it appears that most, if not all, of the research reactors now using HEU can be converted to LEU fuel. If conversion proves impossible in every case, dismantling the handful that remained would seem a small price to pay for complete nuclear disarmament. Similarly, even if it were not possible to convert icebreakers and space reactors (the former are likely to be much easier to convert than the latter), it is difficult to imagine this would be a serious roadblock to disarmament.

Perhaps the biggest barrier to phasing out the production and use of HEU is its use in naval vessels, particularly submarines. Nevertheless, converting naval reactors to run on LEU fuel is possible – France is in the process of converting its vessels for economic reasons. Reports on the enrichment levels in Chinese naval reactors are contradictory, but if they are fuelled with HEU, it is believed that the fuel would be near the 20% enrichment HEU/LEU threshold, and so relatively simple to convert. Similarly, Russian submarines and submarines being developed by India reportedly use fuel with enrichment levels below 45%, making conversion appear feasible. The conversion of naval reactors to LEU fuel does however have two important drawbacks. First, it would almost certainly involve forsaking the 'lifetime cores' (reactors that do not need to be replaced) that are features of the newest British and American submarines. Second, LEU-fuelled reactors are bigger and noisier than HEU-fuelled ones. The second consideration is probably more important than the first to UK and

US policymakers. On balance, however, the barriers to the elimination of HEU seem less daunting than those to the elimination of reprocessing.

Should naval reactors be banned?

A more radical step than ending the use of HEU in naval reactors would to ban naval reactors entirely, including submarine reactors and reactors on aircraft carriers. Article 14 of the Comprehensive Safeguards Agreement (the basic IAEA safeguards agreement) permits states to withdraw from safeguards nuclear material that is for use in 'non-proscribed' military activities – that is, the production of fuel for naval reactors. No state has yet exercised this right (although Canada has considered it), but in a nuclear-weapons-free world, it could represent a significant loophole. States need to consider whether it would be an unacceptable one.

In total, seven nations have built, or are attempting to build, nuclear submarines: the five nuclear-weapons states plus India and Brazil. In addition, a number of other nations, including Canada, Australia and Pakistan, have shown varying degrees of interest in acquiring them. Would these states, or any other non-nuclear-weapons states that might be inclined to consider the use of naval reactors in the future, be prepared to renounce them permanently in order to help bring about a nuclear-weapons-free world as part of a non-discriminatory agreement? Or would they be willing to give international inspectors unprecedented access to some of their most sensitive technologies in order to assuage international concerns? States that possess or are considering the development of nuclear-powered naval vessels should begin to consider options for safeguarding the fuel cycle in a naval context.

CHAPTER FOUR

Enforcement

Chapter 1 posited that before states would proceed over the horizon to prohibit nuclear weapons, they would need to take mutually reinforcing steps to build political confidence, reduce the number and salience of nuclear weapons, and stabilise political and military relations to the point where nuclear weapons did not appear indispensable for preventing war among major powers. Chapter 2 assumed that such steps could be taken, and explored how a prohibition on nuclear weapons might be verified. Chapter 3 suggested ways in which an international expansion of nuclear energy could be reconciled with the elimination of all nuclear arsenals. We now consider how a nuclear-weapons prohibition might be enforced.

Even if near-perfect means existed for verifying a nuclear-weapons ban, a state – or sub-state group – could still fail to comply and dash to acquire nuclear weapons. Nuclear-armed states and their citizens would therefore want to be sure that enforcement of such a ban would be exceptionally reliable before they dismantled their last nuclear weapon.

Curiously, the challenges of enforcing compliance with a nuclear-weapons prohibition have been under-addressed. For example, the Canberra Commission on the Elimination of Nuclear Weapons commissioned by the Australian government in 1995 to 'develop ideas and proposals for a concrete and realistic program to achieve a world totally free of nuclear weapons' acknowledged that 'states must … be confident that any violations detected will be acted upon'. However, in the course of its admirable 120-page report on steps towards a nuclear-weapons-free world, all it has to say about the nature of such enforcement action is that 'the Security Council should continue its consideration of how it might address, consistent with specific mandates given to it and consistent with the Charter of the United Nations, violations of nuclear disarmament obligations'.[1] Proponents of the Model Nuclear Weapons Convention did better in a document that explored the security dynamics that would need to exist for states to comply with such a convention.[2] Their basic conclusion appears both correct and insufficient to encourage states now relying on nuclear-deterrent umbrellas to sign up: 'The stability of a nuclear weapon free regime may depend on the assessment by major powers that it is in their security interests, and on the normative force of the prohibition of acquiring nuclear weapons that would grow as the regime was institutionalised and endured.'[3] In the following discussion we try to sharpen some of the choices that would need to be made in establishing an enforcement system.

There are two distinct challenges in creating enforcement mechanisms strong enough to embolden states to let go of their nuclear umbrellas, one of which is normally glossed over. Firstly, it would be necessary to develop punishments that could deter states from breaching their obligations and deny states the benefits of any violation. This challenge is widely recognised. However, for such punishments to be 'triggered', there must be decision-making avenues and procedures that enjoy international legitimacy and that would work in a manner timely and robust enough to deter or eliminate threats. Most discussions of nuclear disarmament in recent decades have underestimated this second challenge, tacitly assuming that, in the event of a violation, agreed enforcement actions would be employed. Before addressing what appropriate enforcement actions might be, therefore, we explore the various reasons why enforcement might be less than straightforward.

Why enforcing compliance might be contentious

The term 'break-out' evokes images of a state that has covertly acquired nuclear weapons and announces it with a bold, aggressive gambit of blackmail or aggression. Yet this is not the only – or even the most likely – possible type of cheating on a nuclear-weapons prohibition. There is a wide spectrum of non-compliant actions with which an enforcement system might have to contend.

Effective verification should make it possible to detect an attempt to build nuclear weapons before the job is completed and nuclear blackmail or aggression is employed. This is a mixed blessing: if violations were detected some time before weapons were actually produced, the violator (and perhaps its allies) could argue that it had not intended to build nuclear weapons. It could claim that the suspicious activity had peaceful purposes, and was insufficiently declared only by mistake. In a more brazen violation of the rules, it could say it had not intended to actually complete the weapons, but had, for instance, merely sought to warn an adversary to stop its threatening behaviour and to motivate the international community to stop dithering and intervene.

Among other violation scenarios that might present decision-makers with dilemmas about enforcement, what would be the international community's reaction if the inspectorate found evidence that a state had secretly produced polonium-210 (a material that can be used in the initiator of a nuclear weapon), for example, but no evidence of a programme to acquire fissile materials? If the inspectorate discovered a clandestine enrichment facility, but no evidence that it had yet been used to manufacture HEU, would the international community agree on swift punitive sanctions? Iran recently presented similar scenarios.

The room for ambiguity and disagreement over enforcing compliance is great. Bruce Larkin, the author of an 'interpretative encyclopaedia' of nuclear-disarmament-related issues, has identified a number of possible sources of discord, which we list below, along with one addition of our own:

- Disagreement about whether break-out was being accomplished, or even if it was intended.

- Disagreement about whether the action – classic break-out or not – was sufficiently serious to require enforcement.

- Disagreement about the urgency of the enforcement action required (resulting from disagreement about the timescale for break-out).

- Disagreement about whether the means of enforcement to hand would or could be effective.

- Disagreement about the relative importance to be assigned to enforcement, as against other interests that states might have in relation to the alleged violator.

- Concern on the part of some states that a specific enforcement initiative was both unsound in itself and an instrument for enhancing the authority and power of the enforcers.[4]

States would evaluate the seriousness of a non-compliant activity, not only on the basis of the action itself, but also in light of their security, political and economic relations with the alleged violator. There would be a wide spectrum of threat perceptions among states, varying according to the characteristics of both the threatened and the threatening states.

The problem of nuclear 'break-out' is most acute for Israel. Because it is such a small country, even a small number of warheads could pose an existential threat to it. It would therefore certainly fear that it might be annihilated if one of its most belligerent adversaries acquired a small number of nuclear weapons and was not deterrable. Whether this fear would be rational or not is largely immaterial. Israel would not agree to give up its last nuclear weapons unless it were convinced that the threat from its neighbours had diminished profoundly, that enforcement mechanisms were truly effective and that it would have sufficient warning from intelligence to be able to win a break-out race. (There is also the possibility that Israel might decide that it would gain security by offering to give up its nuclear weapons in order to prevent proliferation that would make it less secure. Here, Israel would need to be confident that (i) all the relevant regional states were sufficiently transparent and cooperative that none would seek to acquire or retain WMD; (ii) if they did, they would almost certainly be detected; and (iii) if they were detected, Israel would be able to defeat them itself, or could rely on the US and the international community to deal with the matter effectively.)

At the other end of the spectrum is the United States. Break-out would almost certainly not pose an existential threat to the US because of its size, its conventional power and the technical advantages it enjoys that would probably allow it to reconstitute its nuclear arsenal without too much difficulty. Not only would the US be able to respond to a nuclear attack by conventional means but, more importantly, it might feel able to deter one without its own nuclear weapons because its conventional military (and possibly also its 'cyber', or information-warfare) capabilities mean that it could inflict intolerable damage on any government and on terrorists whom it could locate.[5] On the other hand, if on the path to nuclear abolition the US had attenuated some of its most potent conventional strike capabilities, its capacity to deter and defeat break-out would be diminished. Clearly there is tension between the need to reduce and balance out major powers' conventional capabilities to facilitate nuclear abolition and the need for conventional capabilities to be able to respond to potential violations. In any case, as both a political and psychological matter, the US (like other governments and societies) would be – rightly – unwilling to distinguish between a threat to its existence and, say, a threat to 'only' one or two major cities. The destruction of one or more cities in a scenario in which fears of more such attacks were realistic because the source of threat had not been immediately eliminated might cause the US to react in extreme ways.

Other nuclear-weapons states lie in the middle of the threat spectrum. The United Kingdom is a small country and London, its political and financial centre, holds a significant proportion of the population. A few nuclear weapons of relatively modest yield that destroyed London as a functioning city would seem like an existential threat. The UK, along with France and China, does not have conventional military power-projection capabilities sufficient to give it strong confidence that it could pre-empt or deter an attack from a few illicitly produced nuclear weapons launched on a ballistic missile by a distant adversary.

Before giving up their last nuclear weapons, states would want to feel confident that the risk of even a 'small' break-out was lower than the risk of keeping a small number of nuclear weapons and suffering a failure of nuclear deterrence. Cold-blooded analysts might try to reassure them that break-out would be likely to be detected before any illicit nuclear weapons were produced, and that, at worst, a successful break-out attempt would involve only a minimal number of nuclear weapons, because larger-scale break-out would be detected and interdicted before many deliverable weapons were produced. A nuclear renegade would not for long be able to take and hold territory or otherwise impose its will, because other states would mobilise counterforce, including, if necessary, reconstituted nuclear weapons (reconstitution capabilities are discussed in Chapter 5). Indeed, past experience suggests that nuclear weapons 'work' only to deter or defeat military aggression against their possessor, not as a shield behind which to successfully take and hold territory. Ballistic-missile defences – assuming they were permitted and effective – and advanced air forces could blunt any threat of airborne nuclear attack that the renegade might launch in order to deter efforts to remove him. Conventionally armed missiles and air power could further threaten to negate or at least minimise the renegade's capacity to use a small illegal arsenal. In such a context, the aggressor would be militarily and politically isolated, and the commitment and collective power of the states transgressed against would eventually prevail.

The most probable enforcement problems would be less immediately threatening than the scenario of the renegade leader who attacks another state while announcing to the world that his state has secretly produced nuclear weapons. The medium power breaking a nuclear prohibition in order to deter a larger power from intervening in its territory is one more probable scenario. Most probable of all would be ambiguous non-compliant activities such as the ones over which the UN Security Council has wrestled with Iran. Disagreements over evidence, the seriousness of the alleged non-compliance, the urgency of enforcement and so on could prompt endless rumination and debate among enforcers. Assuming for the moment that the Security Council had an enforcement role, its veto-wielding members – the US, Russia, China, the UK and France – have different allies and friends among states. This raises the prospect that the enforcers might not perceive and respond unanimously to all suspicious activities or violations. For example, if Israel, in the midst of a crisis with an Egyptian government led by the Muslim Brotherhood, were caught secretly producing centrifuges for a new uranium enrichment facility that it said was for peaceful purposes, the US might urge a different international response from that urged by, say, Russia, France or China. If questions arose about Japan's nuclear activities, China might favour a different response from that favoured by the US. Of course, at an abstract and perhaps a moral level, all should be treated equally, but this is not how international politics have tended to operate.

Connecting this back to the theme of Chapter 3, the probability of non-compliance and problems with enforcement is in part determined by how much leeway there is for national nuclear-related activities under the weapons-prohibition regime. The fundamental insight of the Acheson–Lilienthal Plan six decades ago was that the less such leeway there was in the regime, the more difficult it would be for ambiguity about non-compliance to develop and, therefore, for disputes about enforcement to emerge.

The UN Security Council in a nuclear-weapons-free world: relations between China, Russia and the United States

It is difficult to envisage an alternative to the UN Security Council as the body tasked with enforcing a prohibition of nuclear weapons. The P5 would all need to agree for any alternative body to be created. These powers are five of the eight nuclear-armed states, and would prohibit nuclear weapons only on terms they found acceptable. If one or more of them wanted enforcement to reside in the body in which they alone have veto powers, it is impossible to see how an alternative could be imposed on them.

Any consideration of the role of the Security Council as authoriser of the enforcement of a nuclear-weapons prohibition would need to address the issue of the veto. Would states possessing nuclear weapons be willing to eliminate their arsenals knowing that if a P5 member (or an ally of one) were to violate a prohibition on nuclear weapons, the violator or one of its friends could veto enforcement? Alternatively, might the current P5 be willing to relinquish their veto power and their nuclear weapons at the same time? There is no a priori answer to this question, but a bigger leap away from past experience and current politics is required to imagine that the P5 would relinquish the veto than to think that at least one of them would insist on retaining it.

Relationships between the US, China and Russia in the Council are, once again, central. Not only do two of these three states determine the evolution of the largest and most dynamic of the world's nuclear arsenals, but the three together exert substantial influence in the Middle East, Northeast Asia and South Asia, where current and prospective nuclear challenges are greatest. They have been difficult to harmonise on the issues of Iran and – up until around 2006 – North Korea. All the P5 insist that they have no interest in other states acquiring nuclear weapons. Yet in the mid 1990s, when many intelligence services believed that Iraq was not complying fully with UN resolutions mandating its elimination of all WMD capabilities, Security Council members disagreed on how rigorously to enforce compliance. And when confronted with Iran's and North Korea's violations of safeguards agreements, the NPT and Security Council resolutions, the US, China and Russia made substantially different assessments of the degree of threat and the pace and character of measures to seek compliance. China and Russia have consistently been more reluctant than the US both to impose sanctions and to increase their severity once they have been introduced.

Competing national priorities within states could severely complicate the creation and maintenance of a nuclear-weapons-free world. States rarely make decisions on the basis of one factor alone. When non-proliferation objectives conflict with other objectives, it is always necessary to perform some kind of balancing act. US President George Bush, for example, stated in a 2004 election debate with Senator John Kerry that the greatest threat to the US was the proliferation of nuclear weapons. Yet in dealing with the acute proliferation challenges presented by North Korea and Iran, the Bush administration vacillated between favouring regime change and pursuing the diplomatic options preferred by other permanent Security Council members. This raised questions about whether the US in fact had priorities higher than non-proliferation. Similarly, when the US chose to go ahead with its nuclear-cooperation agreement with India in 2005, it assessed that the strategic advantages of a partnership with India would outweigh damage to the NPT.[6] Every state faces such dilemmas – the resistance of China and Russia to dealing more robustly with North Korea and Iran is a consequence of competing Chinese and Russian economic, political and security priorities in relation to those countries.

These are among the issues that would need to be seriously addressed in any deliberations on whether and how to proceed with the total elimination of nuclear weapons and enforce security in a world without them. It is difficult to imagine China, Russia, France, the UK and the US genuinely embarking on a course of nuclear disarmament in the absence of a significant reconciliation of their interests and approaches to regional and global security. If they were willing and able to achieve such reconciliation, enforcement would be much more imaginable. A first-order task, then, is for Beijing, Moscow and Washington to begin discussions of the conditions they think are necessary to establish to begin a genuine transition to a nuclear-weapons-free world. Other states can and should press these three to accept this responsibility.

Adding India, Israel and Pakistan to the mix

If building P5 convergence appears daunting, it would be relatively straightforward compared with winning Indian, Pakistani and Israeli endorsement of mechanisms to bring about a world without nuclear weapons. For the purposes of nuclear disarmament, these states are as important as the P5. But they pose even more complicated challenges. Like other nuclear-armed states, they would not give up their arsenals unless they felt reassured that their security interests would be served in a post-nuclear-weapons environment. Due to their unsettled regional relations, Israel and Pakistan have less confidence in that eventuality than do the US, Russia, China, the UK and France. India, Pakistan and Israel would need to be brought into processes to determine how to manage international enforcement of rules and peaceful relationships well before later steps to eliminate nuclear arsenals could be taken.

India raises the most interesting questions here. It has a history of championing nuclear disarmament. New Delhi might thus be expected to commit to eliminating its nuclear arsenal as and when all other states do. Yet the other nuclear-weapons states should not be surprised if in negotiations on a ban on nuclear weapons, India were to insist on conditions that went to the heart of the international security system. India did not establish the high currency value of nuclear weapons, but since they have gained this coin, why would India not be tempted to bargain its weapons for at least as much power in the international system as its rival China and the less globally important nuclear-armed states, the UK and France? India has long campaigned for a permanent seat on the Security Council. The international response to India's position has been ambivalent for a variety of reasons, among them its non-adherence to the NPT. Nevertheless, in the context of global nuclear disarmament, India should be willing to conform to a new treaty bringing all states into a non-discriminatory regime prohibiting nuclear weapons. It takes no imagination, though, to foresee that if the Security Council were to be the established enforcer of a nuclear-weapons ban, in return for surrendering the security assurances provided by its nuclear weapons, India would want not just a seat but an equal voice – that is, a veto power – in the Council. Balance-of-power concerns and India's political and security relationship with China would make it difficult for any Indian political party to accept a situation in which China had a veto on enforcement matters and India did not.

Attempting to address the disarmament issue together with Security Council reform, including India's quest for permanent admission to the Council, might overload both efforts. Equally, however, India could force the issue by refusing to cooperate in nuclear abolition unless it received a permanent Security Council seat. Pakistan would probably oppose Indian membership of the Council, and might be tempted to seek equal billing, even though it lacks the other attributes that most in the international community associate with valid candidacies for permanent seats. Or else Pakistan might seek to rally other states to oppose Indian permanent membership, thereby placing the disarmament process at risk. Either way, it would be in Pakistan's national interest to try to ensure that it would not be disadvantaged by Indian membership in the body responsible for enforcing nuclear disarmament and international peace and security.

Israel's concerns will probably remain deeply rooted in the region surrounding it, and Israelis are realistic enough to recognise that a bid for permanent membership in the Security Council would be widely rejected and would not be worth seeking. However, before eliminating its nuclear arsenal Israel would insist that the Security Council demonstrated its willingness and ability to enforce resolutions that affected Israel's security. In this sense, Israeli nuclear disarmament would affect and be affected by the role and operation of the Security Council.

In order to avoid the complications associated with Security Council membership, veto rights and so on, leaders of a nuclear-weapons-prohibition effort might propose that the prohibiting treaty or convention establish a separate body to authorise enforcement action. A separate mechanism could strengthen confidence in enforcement by excluding veto powers, and could help to keep the disarmament agenda from being entangled with Security Council reform. The current P5 could retain their cherished veto powers for all matters except those covered by a nuclear-weapons prohibition.

This solution could bring its own problems, however, as the international security system in a world without nuclear weapons could, of course, face non-nuclear threats, some of which would not be easily separable from nuclear ones. Such non-nuclear threats might come from an actor who was also accused of non-compliance with the nuclear ban, or from a party to a regional or global dispute in which non-compliance was alleged against a different party. Would an allegation of nuclear non-compliance always take precedence over other threats to international peace and security? What if the actions authorised by the Security Council and the enforcer of the nuclear-weapons prohibition contradicted each other? With whom would jurisdiction lie? Who would be responsible for disentangling the different elements of threat, conflict and international law, and how would a separate nuclear-enforcement body relate to the Security Council?

Is automatic enforcement the answer?

One possible solution to the problem of enforcement might be to make it automatic. For example, if the proper verification authorities found that a state was trying to acquire nuclear weapons – the specific indicators of which would have been defined in the prohibition process – all states would automatically be mandated to freeze investment in the violator state, or cease arms-supply and other trade relationships with the violator. Penalties would flow from properly established evidence of violation without requiring a vote from any enforcement body.

The question of automatic enforcement would be politically explosive, whether governments agreed to it or not. Past experience would seem to indicate that states would probably insist on leaving room for circumstantial deliberation and negotiations over how to respond to allegations of cheating. They would not want to commit their political authority or their armed forces to potentially dangerous enforcement actions without case-by-case decision-making processes. Yet at the same time, governments engaged in a debate about automatic enforcement who favoured leaving enforcement subject to case-by-case deliberation would be vulnerable to domestic opponents arguing that such an enforcement regime would be too weak to allow the safe elimination of the nuclear deterrent.

Equally, if there were robust automatic-enforcement procedures, domestic opponents might criticise signatory governments for unwittingly setting traps that could be unfairly sprung. They might warn that their own state could be falsely accused, or punished for responding to emerging threats by beginning to reconstitute nuclear capabilities. Politicians imagining such scenarios would tend to oppose an automatic-enforcement regime. There are further pragmatic reasons why states might prefer to retain case-by-case discretion: if one of the most economically and militarily powerful states in the international system were found to be non-compliant with an element of a nuclear-weapons-prohibition agreement, and embargoes on that state were automatic, erstwhile investor states might fear economic retribution from the violator, or worse. Automaticity might give them an excuse – 'we had no choice but to sanction you' – but it would not necessarily dissuade the powerful state from retaliating.

For all these reasons, it would probably not be possible for a consensus to be reached on establishing robust automatic-enforcement measures against non-compliant actors. Even in the event of the co-evolution of political confidence-building, conflict resolution and incremental steps toward nuclear abolition, the more powerful states in the international system would probably want to retain discretion over when and how to act against non-compliance. In other words, enforcement would essentially depend on relations among major powers. Moreover, the possibility would remain that the most powerful states would act unilaterally or in coalitions against a non-compliant state if the established authorising body was unwilling or unable to decide to act. Concern about this possibility would doubtless feature prominently in any deliberations on whether to undertake a nuclear-weapons prohibition and, if one were agreed, on how to enforce it. To sharpen these issues and clarify the key questions, think tanks and experts from interested states should be encouraged to collaborate in exploring them.

Enforcement mechanisms: sanctions and punishments after break-out

Contemporary analysts generally agree that the enforcement procedures for dealing with non-compliance with a nuclear-weapons ban should be essentially the same as those associated with existing treaties, only surer. The Security Council (or whichever body was tasked with enforcing nuclear disarmament) would begin by demanding clarification of suspect activities and an end to non-compliance. Nuclear cooperation with the non-compliant state could be suspended, and other forms of diplomatic pressure and isolation brought to bear. Economic sanctions could be imposed, with graduated degrees of severity. Military sales and cooperation could be curtailed. Some analysts suggest that a nuclear-weapons prohibition would be so important that its violators should be expelled from all international organisations. Ultimately, military action could be taken to end non-compliant activities and/or to destroy threatening capabilities, or, *in extremis*, to remove a threatening government.

Decisions on each of these issues would depend heavily on how the eight nuclear-armed states and other key actors resolved the enforcement-authorising dilemmas discussed above. If the major actors could not agree on the key questions of who should decide on enforcement, whether and how veto power should be retained and the degree of automaticity involved, the application of particular enforcement tools would be too fraught with doubt for states to be motivated to complete nuclear disarmament. Even if robust enforcement procedures could be agreed, decisions on which particular measures to adopt might still be complicated by disagreements of the kind reviewed earlier. Again, the necessity of major-power cooperation reasserts itself – the most difficult enforcement measures to enact would be those against the more powerful states and their friends and allies.

The debate on the effectiveness of enforcement action has often been dominated by the question of whether sanctions or constructive engagement is more appropriate. But the crucial point is not whether, in a given circumstance, a particular kind of enforcement action would be the right response. It is that unless the US, Russia, China, France, the UK, India, Pakistan and Israel each had confidence that agreed enforcement actions would be implemented in the circumstances that it worried about the most, it would not give up its last nuclear weapons. Furthermore, these states would need to be convinced that enforcement would be timely, that the standard of proof required to justify enforcement action would not be so high that it could not in practice be met, and that enforcement would be effective. Words to this effect in a treaty would not, by themselves, be enough to build confidence.

Fortunately, the early steps in preparing the conditions for eliminating nuclear arsenals – including the strengthening of non-proliferation rules and their enforcement – would provide the permanent members of the Security Council with ample opportunity to show each other and the rest of the world whether or not they could make the Council an effective enforcement body. If they failed to cooperate on these early steps, the process of negotiating or implementing a prohibition on nuclear weapons would stop.

Should states be permitted to withdraw from an agreement to abolish nuclear weapons?

Article X of the NPT, on withdrawal from the treaty, permits a state to withdraw 'if it decides that extraordinary events, related to the subject matter of this Treaty, have jeopardized the supreme interest of its country'. Debate about this provision centres on the issue of what might be called 'dishonourable withdrawal' – cases in which a state leaves the NPT to avoid fulfilling its treaty obligations.[7] Examples of dishonourable withdrawal would include the scenario in which a state leaves the treaty only after being found in non-compliance (as North Korea did), or when a state acquires nuclear material and technology, ostensibly for peaceful purposes under Article IV of the treaty, but then withdraws and uses it to develop nuclear weapons. All states today concede that withdrawal from the NPT is a sovereign right, providing it is exercised honourably (although they are notably vague in delineating precisely what this excludes in practice).

A crucial question is whether a similar right to 'honourably' withdraw should exist in an agreement to abolish nuclear weapons. The absence of a withdrawal provision would not be unprecedented. For instance, the 1925 Geneva Protocol prohibiting the use of chemical and biological weapons (to use modern terminology) has no withdrawal clause. The rationale for not including one in an agreement to abolish nuclear weapons is strong: the withdrawal of any one state from the treaty would prejudice the interests of all the others. Moreover, because a nuclear-weapons prohibition would be universal and non-discriminatory, unlike the NPT regime, the justification for a withdrawal option would be weaker, and the consequences of withdrawal graver. While under the NPT, five states possess nuclear weapons that make them able to balance or override the power of a state withdrawing from the treaty, under a universal prohibition such ready-made balancing would not exist.

All recent arms-control agreements have, however, contained a withdrawal clause. For states to be willing to forgo one they would need to be convinced that the Security Council was willing and able both to (i) prevent other states from illegally leaving an abolition agreement and (ii) protect their vital interests so that they would have no need to withdraw themselves. Even if both these conditions were met, national leaders might still be reluctant to sign up to an agreement without a withdrawal clause, partly out of a natural tendency to hedge and partly, as always, out of sensitivity to domestic opinion.

A more viable alternative to excluding the withdrawal option might be to permit withdrawal, but only in certain circumstances and with very stringent conditions attached. To this end, a number of the proposals that have been made with respect to Article X of the NPT in recent years could prove valuable.[8] For instance, in order to increase the political costs of withdrawal, the conditions under which withdrawal from an abolition agreement was permitted could be specified in detail, and the procedure for submitting a notice to withdraw be made to require extensive consultation and discussion.

However, it would probably be necessary to go further and build in explicit protections against the problem of 'dishonourable' withdrawal. To build confidence that states that violated an abolition agreement could not then abandon it, withdrawal could be explicitly forbidden in circumstances in which a state had been found in non-compliance with any of its obligations. It would also be important to ensure that a state had not begun a secret nuclear-weapons programme prior to withdrawal. In the context of the NPT, former US Assistant Secretary of State Robert Einhorn has suggested that if a state wishes to withdraw, it should have to submit to 'highly intrusive verification measures similar to those imposed on Iraq in the fall of 2002'.[9] Although it appears unlikely that states would agree to this provision today, they might do so as part of an agreement to abolish nuclear weapons. Finally, there is the scenario in which a state that has withdrawn makes military use of nuclear material and equipment that it previously acquired under a nuclear-cooperation agreement. A proposal made for the NPT by former IAEA Deputy Director General for Safeguards Pierre Goldschmidt could be adapted to address this possibility – nuclear cooperation could be made contingent on the recipient state agreeing, either to forgo its right to withdraw from the nuclear-weapons ban, or to place all material and equipment under safeguards that would remain even if it did withdraw.[10]

Specifying in detail conditions for withdrawal and the consequences of abusing the right to withdraw would probably be more acceptable to states than eliminating the right entirely. Moreover, because determining the conditions for withdrawal would involve long and detailed discussions, as well as explicit treaty text on withdrawal and enforcement, a withdrawal clause might – perhaps paradoxically – help to build confidence in the viability of the overall abolition agreement. In any event, it is certainly an issue that states should discuss. The recent efforts of NPT review conferences to clarify the procedures for and consequences of withdrawal from that treaty are a helpful start. These might gain momentum if the context were broadened from non-proliferation to disarmament. If nuclear-weapons states were to clearly express a genuine interest in creating conditions for nuclear disarmament, they might be more persuasive in arguing that to make disarmament feasible, states must be prevented from manipulating the non-proliferation regime by reaching the threshold of nuclear-weapons acquisition and then withdrawing.

Prospects for enforcement

Discussions on enforcing a prohibition on nuclear weapons cannot escape the shadows that current conditions and recent history cast over our imaginations. Key states do not yet have the leadership or the relations with other states that would be needed to make an enforceable prohibition of nuclear weapons appear practicable. Any well-informed analyst can cite dozens of obstacles and complications standing in the way of the establishment of means to authorise and implement enforcement that would make states now reliant on nuclear deterrence feel able to relinquish their weapons. Yet it is also possible to take a broader view. Speaking to a conference on nuclear disarmament in Oslo in February 2008, former US Secretary of State George Shultz offered an important rejoinder to pessimism on this issue. Few in the early 1980s, he observed, imagined the political changes that would in a few years result in the peaceful end of the Cold War. Similarly, today, we underestimate the potential for developments that would profoundly change the prospects for abolishing nuclear weapons. If, Shultz suggested, a few leaders of nuclear-armed states stepped forward with conviction and determination to seek the prohibition of nuclear weapons, many obstacles that seem immovable today might become movable.[11] The imperatives that currently motivate working-level officials to impede progress towards abolition would be replaced by imperatives to find solutions that allow movement ahead. The foregoing pages have highlighted the importance of leadership by the US, Russia and China. If leaders in these states could reassure each other on key points and establish an agenda for cooperative security, they could create momentum for stabilising relations in Northeast Asia, South Asia and the Middle East in ways that could prevent further proliferation and facilitate step-by-step nuclear disarmament. Through such evolutionary change led from the top of the nuclear hierarchy, the enforcement challenges that currently appear diffuse and overwhelming would become sufficiently defined to allow negotiations in ensuing years. Whether agreement could then be reached and implemented, no one can say, but the possibility that it might be cannot be denied.

CHAPTER FIVE

Hedging and Managing Nuclear Expertise in the Transition to Zero and After

Even if the nuclear-armed states were to destroy their nuclear weapons, raze their weapons complexes to the ground and submit their fissile material to IAEA safeguards, they would still, by dint of the expertise of their weapons scientists, engineers and process workers, retain a much greater ability than other states to manufacture nuclear weapons. Some nuclear hedging – that is, retention of a capability to reverse the renunciation of nuclear weapons – would be inevitable. Postures might be relatively 'passive', with lead-times to nuclear-weapons re-acquisition of at least several months (rather than a few weeks), but would represent hedging nonetheless.

It is possible that hedging might be seen as an important element of an enforcement regime, at least for a transitional period. Even if states made dramatic progress in devising the reliable verification mechanisms and robust enforcement procedures necessary to enable secure nuclear disarmament, nuclear-armed states – and states that have found security through extended nuclear deterrence – might insist, at least for an intermediate period, on retaining the capacity to reconstitute nuclear arsenals. The desire to hold on to some such capacity is likely to be at least as strong in democracies as in non-democracies, with opposition parties and lobby groups in democracies liable to challenge any government that appeared ready to agree to eliminate the last nuclear weapons. It would be easy for opposition groups to exploit public wariness about disarmament by decrying the absence of a robust capability to reconstitute nuclear forces rapidly; governments might well be inclined to pre-empt such criticisms by making reconstitution capabilities a condition of agreeing to multilateral disarmament. It is no accident that the only country to have eliminated a home-made nuclear arsenal, South Africa, made this move in secret. The states that abandoned their nascent nuclear-weapons activities after 1970 also did so without democratic debate, with the partial exception of Brazil.[1] Judging from past experience, nuclear-weapons laboratories and their patrons would probably also be inclined to push to retain extensive technical and human infrastructure, whatever the strategic pros and cons. Once one nuclear-weapons state insisted on hedging, others would either follow suit or refuse to complete the elimination of their arsenals.

In this chapter, we consider the problems of the transitional phases shortly before and after the last nuclear weapons in national arsenals are dismantled. We discuss the desirability or otherwise of hedging, and consider how nuclear know-how could be managed – an issue that will need to be addressed whether or not hedging is ultimately deemed to be desirable. The management of nuclear knowledge has not received much attention in the past, but it is a subject that would need to receive adequate consideration before nuclear disarmament were undertaken – not least so that after disarmament were completed, the former nuclear-armed states could not be accused by the non-nuclear-weapons states, or each other, of retaining illicit capacity in the form of expertise.

An internationally controlled nuclear deterrent and/or retaliation force?

Because of the difficulties associated with the final leap from low numbers of nuclear weapons to zero and the possible danger of a break-out attempt, the international community would need to consider how it would confront a state that had illicitly retained or acquired nuclear weapons in a world that was otherwise free from them.

Several authors have suggested that, as the nuclear-armed states moved towards zero, they should hand control of some or all of their nuclear weapons over to an international body (which would require an amendment to the NPT or the subordination of the NPT to a nuclear-weapons-prohibition treaty). The concept is that the weapons thus deposited would help to deter any nuclear-armed state from seeking an advantage by refusing to give up its last few warheads, and other actors from seeking to acquire nuclear-weapons capabilities. The international body would have the authority to use its nuclear weapons, but only in the most extreme of circumstances. The detailed model proffered by US analyst Roger Speed involves the creation of an international nuclear deterrent force in stages.[2] Initially, states that possessed nuclear weapons would retain them in small numbers, but would cede decisions about their use to the international authority of the UN Security Council. Authorisation of use could only be given by a majority vote of the Security Council, with its permanent members at this point retaining the power of veto. (Speed's proposal was made in 1994 and did not incorporate India, Pakistan and Israel.) At a final stage, the states possessing nuclear weapons would transfer their remaining arsenals to an international nuclear deterrent force, taking them beyond national control. The operators of the international force, reporting to the Security Council, would maintain these forces and manage their targeting.

Setting aside operational details, which would be exceptionally complex to negotiate, the central problem of this proposal is plausibility. In a world of competing nation-states, it is difficult to envisage any nuclear-armed state handing over control of its nuclear weapons to an international body. Speed argues that an international nuclear force would be retained only to 'deter and possibly retaliate against an outlaw state that has covertly hidden or developed nuclear weapons', and that for this specific function, the permanent members of the Security Council would surrender their veto powers. But regardless of whether or not the veto were retained, each disarming state – including India, Pakistan and Israel – would almost certainly demand an equal voice in any international body managing a centralised arsenal. Many non-nuclear-weapons states might baulk at the idea of internationally controlled nuclear weapons. They might worry about the command-and-control arrangements for such weapons, and fear that, unlike national governments, an international body would actually use them. Others might have the opposite concern – that an international body would be so unlikely to use nuclear weapons that their deterrent value would be lost, making its possession of them pointless.

A truly internationally controlled nuclear deterrent force would only be feasible – and, indeed, desirable – if the eight nuclear-armed states had such mutual confidence that they would be willing to hand control of their nuclear arsenals to other actors and, in the case of the P5, to give up their exceptional power of veto in international-security decision-making. This would be a world in which the perceived need to hedge against uncertainties in the international-security environment had been so reduced that almost all the problems for which nuclear weapons are supposed to be a solution would have been resolved. Because this is an exceptionally distant prospect, the hedges that the nuclear-armed states would be likely to seek instead would be national 'virtual' arsenals or 'surge' capabilities, to which we now turn.

Weapons reconstitution: virtual arsenals and surge capabilities

A more likely hedging scenario than an international nuclear deterrent force would be one in which states retained some capabilities to reconstitute nuclear weapons to deter or retaliate against break-out. Famously, in 1984, US journalist and nuclear analyst Jonathan Schell made a detailed case for 'virtual' nuclear arsenals, or 'weaponless deterrence', as he called it.[3] In his proposal, nuclear-armed states would keep the capability to produce nuclear weapons at very short notice (for instance, in a matter of weeks), instead of the weapons themselves. To enable this, the nuclear-armed states would maintain stockpiles of fissile material, trained workers and production facilities on the point of readiness. In the event of a break-out, the 'virtually' nuclear-armed states would be able quickly to reconstitute their nuclear arsenals in order to oppose the aggressor. Many different models for a reconstitution capability can be imagined, depending on exactly which facilities, materials and personnel the nuclear-armed states were permitted to keep. These factors would affect the amount of time required to produce a (presumably small) operational nuclear force. The minimal capability required for more passive hedging postures, in which the lead time was months rather than weeks, might be termed a 'surge capability'. The exact details of any reconstitution capability would of course need to be specified in negotiations.

The existence of virtual arsenals with a short lead-time might help to deter break-out. If deterrence failed, real nuclear weapons could be reconstituted in an effort to realign the strategic balance. Short-lead-time virtual arsenals might also prevent a proliferation free-for-all, by making it less likely that the allies of erstwhile nuclear-weapons states would seek to acquire nuclear weapons. Because of their longer lead-times, however, it is not clear that surge capabilities would also have this effect.

One possible advantage of legitimising virtual nuclear arsenals or surge capabilities would be that it might make the nuclear-armed states more willing to pursue disarmament in the first place. Indeed, US Special Representative for Nuclear Non-Proliferation Christopher Ford stated in 2007 that 'the potential availability of countervailing reconstitution would need to be a part of deterring "breakout" from a zero-weapons regime'. Ford also remarked that 'this possibility has been incorporated explicitly into US nuclear weapons planning as a way to provide a "hedge" against a technical surprise or geopolitical risk'.[4] The assumption of a hedging option has contributed to the willingness of the US to reduce its – still enormous – nuclear arsenal. The security logic behind reconstitution capabilities and the political motivation to make sure they existed would be even more powerful if the US were thinking seriously about joining or leading a global effort to eliminate all nuclear arsenals.

Virtual nuclear arsenals are, nonetheless, a controversial idea. There are feasibility questions: given that weapons establishments are worried even today about the loss of expertise and the difficulty of recruiting and retaining skilled staff, for how long would they be in a position to deploy the human, financial and technical resources necessary to maintain effective virtual nuclear arsenals in a denuclearising world? Might virtual arsenals be vulnerable to attack, including from the conventional arsenals of an advanced military power? For Schell's concept of weaponless deterrence to work, it must be effectively impossible for one state to destroy another's nuclear-weapons complex. Schell envisages that, in the event of rearmament, nuclear-weapons-production facilities could be dispersed to reduce their vulnerability. However, he also argues at other points that intrusive inspections would be required to ensure that these facilities were not being used to produce nuclear weapons. Such inspections would necessarily reveal the facilities' location, potentially making them vulnerable to destruction by an enemy before they could be dispersed.

Furthermore, there are reasons to worry that virtual nuclear arsenals would foster instability. Schell sees virtual arsenals as a way of preventing the use of nuclear weapons by giving states some degree of genuinely flexible response to major threats. The problem with giving states this option, however, is that they might use it. For instance, during a crisis, a virtual nuclear-weapons state might try to signal its resolve by beginning to reconstitute its nuclear arsenal, which might then provoke a capable adversary, or a belligerent state's security patron, to race to balance it. The potential crisis instability of virtual arsenals has led defence expert Michael Quinlan, for example, to conclude that as a long-term posture, having a few states with modest nuclear arsenals of low political–military salience would give more stable global security than would the existence of only virtual arsenals.

Other criticisms are political. The nuclear potency afforded to disarming states by reconstitution capabilities could undermine the principle of global nuclear equity championed by the many non-nuclear-weapons states dissatisfied with the current nuclear order. Moreover, for many states, nuclear disarmament is not only about equity in an abstract sense, it is also a practical means of reducing the relative power of the US to intervene unilaterally or in small coalitions of its allies and friends around the world. For others, an objective of disarmament is to lessen Russian and Chinese regional assertiveness by removing the emboldening power of their nuclear weapons. In one sense, virtual arsenals would be consistent with the formal abolition of nuclear weapons, and states would no longer be able to use such weapons at very short notice. However, given that the whole purpose of the substitution of virtual nuclear weapons for real ones is to maintain some of the latter's deterrent value, a 'virtual' arrangement would probably not be seen as equitable. Furthermore, because the nuclear-armed states could reconstitute their arsenals in days or weeks, disarmament on these terms would hardly be irreversible. On the other hand, virtual nuclear arsenals could be approached as simply another step on the road to 'genuine' abolition (in the same way that the reduction of numbers of nuclear weapons from thousands to hundreds is). Viewed in this way, they might be seen as more legitimate than the possession of actual arsenals, and hence acceptable for some finite period.

Such questions as these can be resolved only through discussion and, ultimately, negotiation. Once again, there is an imperative for genuine international discussion and debate; taking nuclear disarmament seriously means acknowledging that the states that now possess nuclear weapons would probably insist on retaining, at least for some time, virtual arsenals to deter break-out or retaliate in the event of failure to enforce a nuclear-disarmament regime. These states and leading non-nuclear-weapons states should address this issue head on. To facilitate such deliberations and demonstrate their disarmament bona fides, the NPT nuclear-weapons states should task their nuclear establishments with beginning to model what sorts of reconstitution capabilities would make them most secure in a nuclear-weapons-free world, and what verification arrangements would be needed to ensure that real nuclear weapons were not being produced. The modelling should look beyond unilateral considerations (which are currently the main focus of research in the US) and explore multilaterally what sorts of reconstitution capabilities states would find tolerable in each other, and more or less stabilising. Non-nuclear-weapons states should encourage such modelling and discussions by publicly recognising that states that participate are taking an important step to comply with their disarmament obligations.

Managing residual know-how

Even if reconstitution capabilities were ultimately agreed to be undesirable, it would be inevitable that inequalities between former nuclear-armed states and non-nuclear-weapons states would exist in a nuclear-weapons-free world for at least some time after nuclear weapons had been abolished. Dismantling nuclear weapons and destroying their associated infrastructure would not destroy the nuclear know-how that nuclear-armed states currently possess. It would be impossible to conclusively verify that states had not retained some sensitive documentation, just as it is impossible now to verify the extent of the distribution of the nuclear-weapon designs sold by the A.Q. Khan network. In any case, much nuclear knowledge is embodied in scientists, engineers and other workers.

As destruction of the knowledge embodied in people rather than documents would not be possible – at least, not without committing gross violations of human rights – the knowledge of former nuclear-weapons workers would need to be managed in some way. One aspect of verification that would be peculiar to the transitional period would be verifying the activities of these workers. Many scientists are likely to continue their careers in civilian research establishments, and monitoring their publications would be a useful first step. More intrusive monitoring would provide added reassurance that nuclear-weapons designers and engineers had not resumed their old careers, but this would conflict with privacy rights. What could be done about process workers trained in how to fabricate nuclear weapons and their components? Would their activities need to be monitored, and, if so, how would this be done practically, and without harm to civil liberties? Measures discussed earlier that would make it an international crime for individuals to contribute to the proliferation of nuclear weapons and which would require states in a nuclear-weapons-free world to legally oblige citizens to report evidence of a violation to an international body might help to deter individuals with sensitive expertise from participating in break-out schemes. These are issues that would require careful international examination as part of any serious movement in the direction of nuclear disarmament.

Nuclear know-how would be even more difficult to manage if reconstitution capabilities were retained. But if and when states reached the point where they decided no longer to employ cadres of nuclear-weapons experts, the problem of lingering nuclear know-how might not last indefinitely. There is evidence to suggest that 'tacit' knowledge – in the words of sociologists Donald MacKenzie and Graham Spinardi, 'knowledge that has not been (and perhaps cannot be) formulated explicitly and, therefore, cannot be effectively stored or transferred entirely by impersonal means' – plays an important role in the manufacture of nuclear weapons (which might, incidentally, be another reason why the 'nuclear weapons cannot be disinvented' mantra is misleading).[5] MacKenzie and Spinardi give the example of the manufacture of nuclear-weapon components. Even in an age of computer-controlled machine tools, highly skilled machinists are still needed to manufacture components of sufficient quality for use in nuclear weapons. Artisanal skills such as these can only be learnt 'on the job'; reading an instruction manual will not suffice. Were a generation of machinists to die without training replacements, future generations would, in a real sense, have to reinvent their skill.

If this concept of tacit knowledge is indeed relevant to nuclear weapons, the transitional phase for nuclear know-how could reasonably be said to last for as long as the final generation of nuclear-weapons designers, engineers and process workers remained alive; it would also imply that verifying the destruction of all documentation on nuclear-weapons design was not of paramount importance. The transitional period could be shortened if the nuclear-armed states were to wind down their nuclear-weapons programmes for some years before disarmament by not making new appointments, and retaining only a skeleton staff sufficient to ensure the safety of the few remaining weapons. After the transitional phase, the former nuclear-armed states would find it as difficult as any other state to build nuclear weapons. Reconstruction would still be possible, but some lost tacit knowledge would need to be rediscovered.

CONCLUSIONS

The preceding pages are intended to be a contribution to the long and detailed international discussion that will be needed if nuclear weapons are to be prohibited. We have tried to define and briefly consider challenges of three broad types. Some are technical, such as the questions of how the dismantlement of nuclear warheads could be verified, and whether declared inventories of fissile materials can be monitored with high confidence. More are political–technical, for instance, whether national or multinational control over fuel-cycle facilities would give greater confidence that break-out from a nuclear-weapons prohibition could be avoided. The third type of challenge is purely political: the majority of the issues we have addressed fall into this category. Because verification cannot provide perfect assurance that all violations would be detected in a timely manner, and in any case cannot in itself prevent break-out, enforcement would be a crucial factor in determining whether a prohibition of nuclear weapons would work and whether it would make the world safer than it would be if nuclear weapons were retained and the risk of proliferation remained at least as great as today.

We conclude by addressing some of the political issues that might be raised as the various difficulties involved in securely prohibiting nuclear weapons are confronted. One simple reaction to the entire project might be 'why bother?'. Proponents of nuclear weapons say, 'Nuclear weapons preserve the peace; getting rid of them is a bad idea even if you could verify and enforce disarmament.' Others say, 'Abolition is more trouble and cost than it's worth, and states are not going to cooperate enough to make enforcement reliable. Nuclear disarmament is not practicable enough to take seriously.' Some in non-nuclear-weapons states might make a similar point from a different angle: 'The nuclear-armed states are going to place a multitude of demands and conditions on the non-nuclear-weapons states, and then at the end they will find an excuse to keep some of their weapons anyway, so why bother supporting them in their disarmament? We should get as much nuclear technology as we can without accepting any new limits on our rights. Let the big powers worry about proliferation, but don't expect us to help with sanctions or support of military force.'

Clearly, nuclear-armed states would demand a great deal from each other and from many non-nuclear-weapons states in creating the conditions that would reassure them that they would not be worse off without their nuclear arsenals. The nuclear 'haves' would feel that they had leverage over the 'have-nots', because they possessed something that the others wanted them to give up. If non-nuclear-weapons states did not accept their demands, they would, in effect, shrug their shoulders and say 'fine, we'll keep our weapons then'. (Though this attitude would presumably change if a nuclear weapon were deliberately or accidentally detonated, provoking an international clamour for disarmament.)

Non-nuclear-weapons states might for their part have little time for the concerns of nuclear-armed states, and would resent being expected to do more to help these states feel safe enough to relinquish their weapons. Most non-nuclear-weapons states already live with the vulnerability to external aggression that the states with nuclear weapons use their arsenals to minimise. 'Welcome to the club' might be a common response from non-nuclear-weapons states to the worries of those contemplating giving up their nuclear arsenals.

But firm leaders would be needed in the non-nuclear-weapons states to enable these states to resist the temptation to regard disarmament as a problem for the nuclear 'haves' alone. Accompanying the political–psychological morality play of nuclear states' disarmament would be the reality that when the nuclear powers feel insecure, non-nuclear-weapons states can suffer the consequences. A conventional war in the Taiwan Strait would impose severe dangers and costs on Japan and much of East Asia, and cause enormous global economic suffering (although the harm done by nuclear war could be many times greater). A conventional war involving a non-nuclear Israel might well be difficult to contain; the violence could spread throughout the Middle East, with global economic shocks resulting from interruptions in energy flows. (Though, similarly, the consequences of nuclear detonations in the region could be even more pernicious and long-lasting.) In a global society and economy, no state is an island. If nuclear disarmament resulted in acute instability in relations among major powers, all states would become more vulnerable as a result. Therefore – regardless of the fairness or otherwise of this situation – non-nuclear-weapons states would be wise to be responsive to the reasonable expectations of nuclear-armed states trying to create conditions for the secure prohibition of nuclear weapons.

Equally, nuclear-armed states are unfair, politically unwise and even dangerously insouciant if they think that nuclear abolition merits little more than fine words and the occasional gesture. We offer briefly here five reasons why the objective should be taken more seriously than it has been in the past.

By bringing the NPT into force, the nuclear-weapons states were promising eventually to eliminate their nuclear arsenals. Although some dispute this interpretation of the treaty, the nuclear-weapons states themselves explicitly reaffirmed this undertaking at the 1995 Review and Extension Conference; had they not done so, the treaty would probably have been extended only for a limited time, with its future dependent on more stringent adherence to nuclear-disarmament benchmarks. Such commitments as these must be taken seriously if a rules-based international system is to be upheld. The alternative is a breakdown of nuclear order and a more precarious effort to manage it through competition and perhaps warfare.

The expansion of nuclear energy will threaten security if it is not paired with the universal adoption of tougher verification and inspection protocols and other instruments, such as new rules for managing the nuclear fuel-cycle. Some commentators, including former US Defense Secretary Harold Brown, emphasise the need for agreements to inhibit the acquisition of capabilities to produce weapons-grade fissile material, while arguing against making the abolition of nuclear weapons a 'driving goal'.[1] However, there is little basis for believing that agreement on the new rules advocated by Brown and others will be obtained if non-nuclear-weapons states are not motivated to adhere to such rules. Key non-nuclear-weapons states say that motivation is undermined by the failure of the nuclear-armed few to work in good faith towards fulfilling the disarmament bargain. Seriously pursuing disarmament is therefore necessary to prevent proliferation and make the probably inevitable expansion of nuclear energy safe. At the same time, however, non-nuclear-weapons states should realise that they will get neither the nuclear industry nor the disarmament they seek if they fail to join efforts to strengthen and enforce the non-proliferation regime.

Preventing nuclear terrorism is another major reason to pursue the measures necessary to securely and verifiably eliminate nuclear arsenals and enforceably bar proliferation. If such measures are not pursued, and nuclear arsenals and the production of fuel for them continue, the risk of proliferation to nuclear terrorists will grow with time. (The terrorism-prevention benefits of many of the arms-reduction, nuclear-fuel-cycle management and verification measures described here would accrue even if the last steps from small arsenals to zero nuclear weapons were not completed.)

The failure of the nuclear-armed states to eliminate their nuclear arsenals is likely to tempt others to seek their own such weapons in coming decades. So long as some continue to place great value on and derive power and status from nuclear weapons, others will want their own share in this currency. In addition, the nuclear arsenals of some states prompt other states to seek balancing capabilities for status, to deter coercion and to preserve their territorial integrity against the greater power. The power projection that weaker states seek to deter may not involve nuclear weapons, but the fact that the states most likely to undertake interventions in other countries possess nuclear weapons helps to provide a political justification for proliferation in the name of strategic balancing.[2] For these reasons, a prohibition of nuclear weapons must be pursued today to prevent nuclear competition tomorrow, even if other means of balancing power and resolving security dilemmas will also be necessary.

The ultimate reason for trying to eliminate nuclear arsenals is to reduce the danger of sudden mass annihilation that nuclear weapons are uniquely capable of producing. It is true that if the risk of major war were to increase as a result of nuclear disarmament, the benefit of avoiding the possibility of massive destruction might be overshadowed by the initiation of a period of dire insecurity. But any perception that such a risk was real would prevent the states that now possess nuclear weapons from taking the very last steps to eliminate them. Nor would they abolish their last nuclear weapons if they lacked confidence that effective and reliable mechanisms were in place to deal with unanticipated conflict among major powers.

Before an abolition process can begin, the classic 'who goes first' problem must be resolved. The failure to enforce current non-proliferation rules and norms in respect of Iran and North Korea makes nuclear-armed states reluctant to make serious moves towards eliminating their nuclear arsenals. Doubts about whether it will be possible to agree rules that are clearly needed to reduce proliferation risks as nuclear energy expands would stand in the way of final steps towards the elimination of all nuclear arsenals, even as they should not impede further reductions and other arms-control measures. Yet key non-nuclear-weapons states are reluctant to strengthen non-proliferation rules and their enforcement without action in the field of disarmament. Recent experience shows that insisting on progress in one area before moving in another leads to paralysis. The few actors with uncertain or subversive intentions – Iran and North Korea, most dramatically – exploit this paralysis to move past the guardians of non-proliferation. The only way to remobilise the system is to move on both fronts simultaneously. This requires different strategies from those pursued by world leaders in recent decades.

Ideally, governments of both nuclear-armed and non-nuclear-weapons states would take up this combined non-proliferation and disarmament challenge in the near term. If they are unwilling to do so directly, and are chary of undertaking ambitious negotiations, they would earn political credit for themselves and advance this important international agenda by facilitating an international collaboration of government-affiliated and independent think tanks to explore the conditions necessary for the secure prohibition of nuclear weapons. Governments could encourage private foundations to initiate such a project by making available relevant nuclear-weapons and arms-control experts and military strategists to inform and appraise the deliberations of analysts from think tanks and academia. Going further, governments could then invite participants in such a collaboration to present their conclusions to NPT review meetings, national governments, the Conference on Disarmament and the UN General Assembly.

The nuclear order created in the Cold War, and founded on the NPT, is experiencing entropy just as interest in expanding nuclear energy is rising. Many observers view the 2010 NPT Review Conference as a vital opportunity for renovating the global nuclear order. Encouraging experts from a representative range of states and fields to map possible routes to a nuclear-weapons-free world would be a useful step in this enormous renovation project.

Key Suggestions and Questions

- An international consortium of think tanks should convene a high-level unofficial panel to allow experts from civil society and officials from both nuclear-armed states and non-nuclear-weapons states to explore solutions to the myriad challenges of verifiably and securely eliminating nuclear weapons. Governments could assist these explorations by facilitating the participation of their nuclear-weapons laboratories and militaries.

- To prevent further weakening of the international non-proliferation regime and to enhance the prospects of a safe and secure global expansion of nuclear industry, states must, at a minimum, quickly bring into force the CTBT and agree upon a legal instrument to end further production of fissile materials for weapons. These and other elements of the 13 Steps agreed at the 2000 NPT Review Conference are part of the pathway towards the abolition of nuclear weapons which this Adelphi Paper explores.

Chapter 1

- To enable the project of nuclear disarmament to proceed, the new leaders of the US and Russia should further reduce the size, roles and political–strategic prominence of their nuclear arsenals.

- To give a better sense of how and when a global process of nuclear disarmament might be envisaged, Chinese officials and analysts should begin internal deliberations to specify what level of US and Russian reductions would be sufficient to induce China to join in a disarmament process.

- The nuclear-armed states as a group, and the US and Russia in particular, should reassure the world by agreeing not to routinely deploy nuclear weapons poised for immediate use and vulnerable to destruction if not used on warning of incoming attack.

- The US would need to show a dependable willingness to eschew unilateral or small-coalition military intervention with conventional weapons, in order for others to be persuaded to lay down their nuclear arms and enforce a prohibition on nuclear weapons. However, concerns about strategic intentions and conventional force imbalances in a nuclear-disarmed world should not be allowed to justify a Russian, Chinese or US refusal to reduce nuclear arsenals to low numbers (in the event that the ballistic-missile-defence problem is resolved).

- The US, Russia and China should explore whether and how ballistic-missile defences might stabilise the global nuclear order and help to create conditions for nuclear disarmament.

- The US should deliberate thoroughly with Japan and South Korea and its NATO allies, especially Turkey, to reassure them that US commitments to their security would be no less effective while steps towards nuclear disarmament were being taken.

- To gauge the willingness of the US, Russia, China, India, Pakistan, Israel and others to take nuclear disarmament seriously, and to elaborate the conditions that must be established for them to move in the direction of disarmament, these states should informally explore together their objections to nuclear transparency.

- The disclosure and verification process in North Korea should be valued not only for its immediate contributions to alleviating nuclear insecurity, but also as a test case for future nuclear disarmament.

- Resolving the Iranian nuclear crisis is a necessary political and security condition for allowing evolutionary steps towards regional and global nuclear disarmament.

- The international community should make the illicit proliferation of nuclear weapons and materiel an international crime.

- The challenges of achieving stability and security in a world with much lower total numbers of nuclear weapons should be discussed sooner rather than later by nuclear-armed and non-nuclear-weapons states alike to demonstrate a serious interest in nuclear disarmament.

Chapter 2

- What standard of verification would be required for disarmament? Would states demand near-perfection, would they be satisfied with a 'do-your-best' approach, or could inadequacies in verification be compensated for by a more robust enforcement scheme?

- Would non-nuclear-weapons states trust the verification results achieved using information-barrier technology?

- Could transparency, especially in the form of detailed nuclear histories, compensate for the inevitably inconclusive nature of the results of technical verification? Would non-nuclear-weapons states that had had nuclear-weapons programmes in the past (but not developed actual weapons) need to be transparent about those programmes?

- Would provisions to encourage and protect civil-society monitoring be useful or necessary? If so, what political conditions would be required for it to be effective?

- Nuclear-armed states should appoint national commissions to record the histories of their nuclear-weapons programmes (even if these histories were to remain classified for the time being). States should also discuss among themselves standards for record-keeping and archiving.

- Nuclear-armed states, the US and Russia in particular, should demonstrate prototype end-to-end schemes for verifying the dismantling of declared nuclear warheads.

- Nuclear-armed states should undertake further research into disarmament verification. Three key areas for research are (i) information-barrier technology; (ii) procedures for managed access for challenge inspections; and (iii) the question of what currently classified information might in future be made available to inspectors to assist them with verification. Within the constraints of Article I of the NPT, nuclear-armed states should cooperate with non-nuclear-weapons states on these problems (as the UK and Norway have begun to do).

- All the nuclear armed-states should be more transparent about their nuclear programmes, where such transparency would not undermine stability.

- The IAEA and states party to the NPT should agree to make use of 'special inspections'.

Chapter 3

- If key non-nuclear-weapons states are not willing to accept legal restrictions on the spread of enrichment and reprocessing technology, what other steps are they willing to take to build confidence in non-proliferation?

- Given the (political) problems of the enforcement process – in particular, the timelag between the detection of non-compliance and the implementation of enforcement actions – can a system of safeguards designed to detect but not prevent a violation ever build confidence in non-proliferation sufficient to permit complete disarmament?

- Would multinationalisation or internationalisation of the fuel cycle overcome the limitations of traditional safeguards?

- Can the most proliferation-sensitive activities (reprocessing, HEU production and the naval fuel cycle) ever be compatible with a nuclear-weapons-free world?

- More generally, all states should enter into constructive dialogue about how the expansion of nuclear energy can be reconciled with disarmament. In particular, they should explore (i) whether much more intrusive and rigorous IAEA safeguards would be accept-able if implemented on a non-discriminatory basis in the context of disarmament; (ii) the potential for multinational or international control of the fuel cycle; and (iii) the balance of benefits and risks in the most proliferation-sensitive activities.

- IAEA safeguards should be enhanced. Moreover, the Security Council should act on non-compliance much faster and should adopt a more reasonable standard of evidence than proof beyond reasonable doubt to authorise enforcement actions.

- States that have or are developing naval propulsion reactors should begin to devise and assess the feasibility of options for placing the naval fuel cycle under IAEA safeguards.

Chapter 4

- Could nuclear-armed states reconcile the tension between the prob-able need for conventional arms control and other power-balancing measures and the need for robust conventional military capabilities to deter or defeat the most threatening forms of non-compliance with a nuclear-weapons prohibition?

- Given the possibility of ambiguities in cases of alleged non-compliance and disagreements among key states over evidence and appropriate responses, by what means could inspecting agencies and enforcing states assure themselves and the broader international community that enforcement would be timely, fair and effective?

- Given the role of the UN Security Council, and the fact that its current veto-wielding permanent members all possess nuclear weapons, would it be feasible to empower a different body or group of states to enforce a nuclear-weapons prohibition? How would the new body relate to the Security Council in cases where non-compliance was entangled with other threats to international peace and security?

- If the Security Council was to be the principal enforcement body, would the current P5 retain veto powers? What would be the impli-cations if they did or did not?

- How could India, Pakistan and Israel – nuclear-armed states without permanent membership in the Security Council – be integrated into mechanisms for enforcing a nuclear-weapons prohibition? What form of participation would each be likely to demand as a condition of agreeing to eliminate its nuclear arsenal?

- Experts and officials from nuclear-armed states should explore, perhaps in collaboration with think tanks, the pros and cons of automatic enforcement mechanisms for responding to non-compliance with a nuclear-weapons prohibition. They should also explore whether a prohibition convention should include a right to withdraw, and if so, under what conditions.

Chapter 5

- As the nuclear-armed states brought nuclear-weapons numbers closer to zero, should an international authority be given control over a small stockpile of nuclear weapons? If so, how would such an arrangement work in practice? Who would authorise the weapons' use? Under what circumstances would use be permitted? What would the command and control arrangements be? Would the system be credible enough to deter effectively?

- Would the existence of virtual nuclear arsenals or surge capabilities in place of physical arsenals be an acceptable end point of the disarmament process? If not, would it be acceptable as an interim measure?

- States should begin a discussion about the principle of virtual nuclear arsenals. To facilitate more detailed negotiations later, the nuclear-armed states should begin exploring what would be required for virtual nuclear arsenals to be employed in practice, and the possible effects of such arsenals on strategic stability. Non-nuclear-weapons states should encourage such exploration by publicly recognising that it is a useful step towards disarmament.

- What measures could be taken to build confidence that former nuclear-weapons scientists, engineers and process workers were not using their know-how for proscribed ends?

NOTES

Introduction

1   The authors would like to thank the people who commented on earlier drafts of this paper for their extremely helpful comments.

2   George P. Shultz, William J. Perry, Henry A. Kissinger and Sam Nunn, 'A World Free of Nuclear Weapons', *Wall Street Journal*, 4 January 2007, p. A15; Shultz, Perry, Kissinger and Nunn, 'Toward a Nuclear-Free World', *Wall Street Journal*, 15 January 2008, http://online.wsj.com/article/SB120036422673589947.html.

3   Douglas Hurd, Malcolm Rifkind, David Owen and George Robertson, 'Start Worrying and Learn to Ditch the Bomb', *The Times*, 30 June 2008, http://www.timesonline.co.uk/tol/comment/columnists/guest_contributors/article4237387.ece.

4   Gordon Brown, speech to the Chamber of Commerce, New Delhi, 21 January 2008, http://www.number10.gov.uk/output/Page14323.asp; Margaret Beckett, 'Keynote Address: A World Free of Nuclear Weapons?', Carnegie International Non-Proliferation Conference, Washington DC, 25 June 2007, http://www.carnegieendowment.org/events/index.cfm?fa=eventDetail&id=1004; Des Browne, 'Laying the Foundations for Multilateral Disarmament', Conference on Disarmament, Geneva, 5 February

2008, http://www.mod.uk/defenceinternet/aboutdefence/people/speeches/sofs/20080205layingthefoundationsformultilateraldisarmament.htm.

5   Manmohan Singh, speech to 'Towards a World Free of Nuclear Weapons' conference, New Delhi, 9 June 2008, http://pmindia.nic.in/lspeech.asp?id=688.

6   NPT (1968), Article III.

7   In June 2007, as she suggested steps that might be taken to create the conditions for nuclear disarmament, UK Foreign and Commonwealth Secretary Margaret Beckett remarked that 'the point of doing more on disarmament is this: because the moderate majority of states … want us to do more. And if we do not, we risk helping Iran and North Korea in their efforts to muddy the water, to turn the blame for their own nuclear intransigence back onto us. They can undermine our arguments for strong international action in support of the NPT by painting us as doing too little, too late to fulfil our own obligations.' Beckett, 'Keynote Address: A World Free of Nuclear Weapons?'.

8   Article VI states that 'Each of the Parties to the Treaty undertakes to pursue negotiations in good faith on effective measures relating to cessation of the nuclear arms race at an early date and to nuclear disarmament, and on a treaty on

general and complete disarmament under strict and effective international control.'

9   George Perkovich, Jessica T. Mathews, Joseph Cirincione, Rose Gottemoeller, Jon B. Wolfsthal, *Universal Compliance: A Strategy for Nuclear Security*, 2006 edition

(Washington DC: Carnegie Endowment for International Peace, 2006); William Walker, 'Nuclear Enlightenment and Counter-Enlightenment', *International Affairs*, vol. 83, no. 3, May 2007, pp. 431–53.

Chapter One

1   Tony Blair, 'Parliamentary Statement on Trident', 4 December 2006, www.number-10.gov.uk/output/Page10532.asp.

2   Testimony of General Kevin Chilton to the US Senate Armed Services Committee, 12 March 2008, p. 8, http://www.stratcom.mil/Spch&test/CC%20SASC%20testimony%2012%20Marchb08.html. For earlier, similar remarks from Chilton, see 'US Needs Nuclear Weapons for Rest of Century: General', Agence France-Presse, 4 March 2008, http://afp.google.com/article/ALeqM5iTzGwvCk5GwEruTtZjFLeGRjB8Rw.

3   William Walker, correspondence with authors, 22 April 2008.

4   See Singh, speech to 'Towards a World Free of Nuclear Weapons' conference.

5   Robert S. Norris and Hans M. Kristensen, 'Russian Nuclear Forces, 2008', NRDC Nuclear Notebook, *Bulletin of the Atomic Scientists*, vol. 64, no. 2, May–June 2008, pp. 54–7, http://thebulletin.metapress.com/content/t2j78437407v3qv1/fulltext.pdf.

6   Shultz, Perry, Kissinger and Nunn, 'Toward a Nuclear-Free World'.

7   See Luxembourg Conference Declaration, International Conference on Preventing Nuclear Catastrophe, 24–25 May 2007, http://www.pnc2007.org/eng/declaration/declaration/.

8   Nicolas Sarkozy, 'Presentation of SSBM [sic] *Le Terrible*', Cherbourg, 21 March 2008, http://www.ambafrance-uk.org/President-Sarkozy-s-speech-at,10430.html.

9   Rebecca Johnson, 'Is the NPT Up to the Challenge of Proliferation?', *Disarmament Forum*, no. 4. 2004.

10   Author interviews with officials in Washington and London, April, May and June 2007.

11   Sarkozy, 'Presentation of SSBM [sic] *Le Terrible*'. French officials intended this speech, delivered at the launch of a French nuclear submarine, to be the new government's major articulation of France's nuclear policy. For an illuminating analysis of the speech, see Bruno Tertrais, 'France and Nuclear Disarmament: The Meaning of the Sarkozy Speech', Carnegie Proliferation Analysis, 1 May 2008.

12   Blair, 'Parliamentary Statement on Trident'.

13   Des Browne, 'Laying the Foundations for Multilateral Disarmament', statement to the Conference on Disarmament, Geneva, 5 February 2008, http://www.mod.uk/defenceinternet/aboutdefence/people/speeches/sofs/20080205layingthefoundationsformultilateraldisarmament.htm.

14   Larry M. Wortzel, *China's Nuclear Forces: Operations, Training, Doctrine, Command, Control and Campaign Planning* (Carlisle, PA: Strategic Studies Institute, May 2007), p. 16, http://www.strategicstudiesinstitute.army.mil/pubs/display.cfm?pubID=776.

15   Kristensen, 'Chinese Nuclear Arsenal Increased by 25 Percent since 2006, Pentagon Report Indicates', FAS Strategic Security Blog, 6 March 2008, www.fas.org/blog/ssp/2008/03/chinese_nuclear_arsenal_increa.php/.

16   *Ibid.*

17   Norris and Kristensen, 'India's Nuclear Forces, 2007', NRDC Nuclear Notebook, *Bulletin of the Atomic Scientists*, vol. 63, no. 4, July–August 2007, pp. 74–8, http://thebulletin.metapress.com/content/hm378jxpm12u4342/fulltext.pdf.

18   Shyam Saran, 'Cold Warriors Do A Flip', *Times of India*, 26 February 2008.

19   Norris and Kristensen, 'Pakistan's Nuclear Forces, 2007', NRDC Nuclear Notebook, *Bulletin of the Atomic Scientists*, vol. 63, no. 3, May–June 2007, pp. 71–4, http://thebulletin.metapress.com/content/k4q43h2104032426/fulltext.pdf.

20   Harold Brown, 'New Nuclear Realities', *Washington Quarterly*, vol. 31, no. 1, Winter 2007–08, pp. 7–22, http://www.twq.com/08winter/docs/08winter_brown.pdf.

21   Wortzel, 'China's Nuclear Forces: Operations, Training, Doctrine, Command, Control and Campaign Planning', p. viii.

22   Many states may today assume that US non-nuclear military superiority will continue indefinitely, but it should be remembered that history records the sudden decline of a number of great powers. American national-security officials and analysts may therefore worry about the durability of American military primacy in a world without nuclear weapons, as might states that now rely on US security guarantees. This concern should not, however, be used as an argument against prohibiting nuclear weapons. The US and its current allies and friends could prepare for a comparative decline in American power by devoting greater effort now to building regional security regimes in Northeast Asia and the Gulf, and with Russia on the southern and eastern flanks of Europe. In view of recent experience in the Balkans and Iraq, and in dealing with North Korea – and taking account of rising transnational challenges such as climate change, terrorism and organised crime – the high value placed on kinetic military power in US thinking about national and international security will need to be reconsidered in any case. The most pressing security challenges today – in Iraq, Afghanistan, Pakistan, the Middle East, the Balkans, Africa and elsewhere – require pacification and constructive capacities more than destructive ones. As US Defense Secretary Robert Gates has observed, 'Other countries are not going to come at us in a conventional war'. Karen DeYoung, 'Gates: US Should Engage Iran with Incentives, Pressure', *Washington Post*, 15 May 2008, p. A4.

23   This shift is reflected most clearly in private communications with Taiwanese leaders and in the private comments of former high-ranking US officials, including former leaders of Pacific Command. Conversations with author, early 2008.

24   Remarks by former US Deputy National Security Advisor J.D. Crouch in response to presentation by Perkovich to the conference 'The Crisis in Nonproliferation: Meeting the Challenge', American Enterprise Institute for Public Policy Research, Washington DC, 8 April 2008, http://www.aei.org/events/filter.all,eventID.1703/transcript.asp.

25   Human Rights Watch, *Off Target: The Conduct of the War and Civilian Casualties in Iraq* (New York: Human Rights Watch, 2003), p. 23.

26   Sarkozy, 'Presentation of SSBM [sic] *Le Terrible*'.

27   See Wortzel, 'China's Nuclear Forces: Operations, Training, Doctrine, Command, Control and Campaign Planning'.

28   For discussions of possible transparency measures, see for example Gunnar Arbman, 'Nuclear Transparency from the Perspective of Non-Nuclear Weapon States', in Nicholas Zarimpas (ed.), *Transparency in Nuclear Warheads and Materials* (Oxford: Oxford University Press for the Stockholm International Peace Research Institute, 2003); Steve Fetter, 'A Comprehensive Transparency Regime for Warheads and Fissile

Materials', *Arms Control Today*, vol. 29, no. 1, January–February 1999, http://www.armscontrol.org/act/1999_01-02/sfjf99.asp; and 'Reporting by States Parties', working paper submitted by Canada to the Preparatory Committee for the 2005 Review Conference of the Parties to the Treaty on the Non-Proliferation of Nuclear Weapons, NPT/CONF.2005/PC.III/WP.2, 5 April 2004, http://www.reachingcriticalwill.org/legal/npt/prepcom04/papers/canadawp2.pdf.

29 Reprocessing is the extraction of plutonium from spent fuel.

30 The American author has heard highly respected former senior US officials make this point on many occasions.

Chapter Two

1 The need for perfect verification has been expressed to us on a number of occasions; interestingly, however, we have yet to come across it in print. The closest approximation we have found is Henry Sokolski and Gary Schmitt, 'Advice for Nuclear Abolitionists', *The Weekly Standard*, vol. 13, no. 33, 12 May 2008. That we have heard much talk about the need for perfect verification but have not seen it argued in print seems to us to be a symptom of the tendency of the 'dismissive realists' (to use defence expert Michael Quinlan's term) to reject disarmament out of hand rather than debate it in a serious way.

2 Office of Technology Assessment, US Congress, *Verification Technologies: Cooperative Aerial Surveillance in International Agreements* (Washington DC: US Government Printing Office, July 1991), p. 104, Box C-1, footnote 1, http://www.princeton.edu/~ota/disk1/1991/9114/9114.PDF.

3 Allan S. Krass, *Verification: How Much is Enough?* (London: Taylor and Francis for SIPRI, 1985), pp. 167–71.

4 For the argument that small caches would not pose an unacceptable threat, see, for instance, James Leonard, Martin Kaplan and Benjamin Sanders, 'Verification and Enforcement in a NWFW', in Jack Steinberger, Bhalchandra Udgaonkar and Joseph Rotblat (eds), *A Nuclear-Weapon-Free World: Desirable? Feasible?* (Boulder, CO: Westview Press, 1993); for the opposite view, see Charles L. Glaser, 'The Flawed Case for Nuclear Disarmament', *Survival*, vol. 40, no. 1, Spring 1998, pp. 114–16.

5 Krass, *Verification: How Much is Enough?*, p. 169.

6 Conversation with authors, London, November 2007.

7 For an exploration of trust and disarmament, see Ken Booth and Nicholas J. Wheeler, 'Beyond Nuclearism', in Regina Cowan Karp (ed.), *Security Without Nuclear Weapons? Different Perspectives on Non-Nuclear Security* (Oxford: Oxford University Press for SIPRI, 1992).

8 Browne, 'Laying the Foundations for Multilateral Disarmament'.

9 Broadly, this is the position taken in the Model Nuclear Weapons Convention, a draft convention to ban nuclear weapons put together by an international association of nuclear-disarmament advocates. It is the most comprehensive attempt to date to draft such a treaty. See *Securing Our Survival: The Case for a Nuclear Weapons Convention* (Cambridge, MA: International Physicians for the Prevention of Nuclear War, International Association of Lawyers Against Nuclear Arms, International Network of Engineers and Scientists Against Proliferation, 2007), http://www.icanw.org/securing-our-survival.

10 Some plants manufacture a combination of civilian-use and nuclear-weapons-

related technologies. For example, the All Russian Research Institute of Automatics manufactures both initiators for nuclear weapons and portable neutron generators for peaceful purposes such as well-logging (recording the geologic formations around gas and oil wells). See http://www.vniia.ru/eng/ng/index.html.

11   Arms Control Association, 'Worldwide Ballistic Missile Inventories', fact sheet, September 2007, http://www.armscontrol. org/factsheets/missiles.asp.

12   The scheme laid out here is essentially an amalgamation of the proposals put forward in the following works: Committee on International Security and Arms Control, National Academy of Sciences, *Monitoring Nuclear Weapons and Nuclear Explosive Materials: An Assessment of Methods and Capabilities* (Washington DC: National Academies Press, 2005), http:// www.nap.edu/catalog.php?record_ id=11265; 'Verifying Deep Reductions in Nuclear Forces', in Harold A. Feiveson (ed.), *The Nuclear Turning Point: A Blueprint for Deep Cuts and De-Alerting of Nuclear Weapons* (Washington DC: Brookings Institution Press, 1999); Fetter, 'Verifying Nuclear Disarmament', Henry L. Stimson Center, Occasional Paper no. 29, October 1996, http://www.stimson. org/wmd/pdf/fetter.pdf; Edward Ifft, 'Monitoring Nuclear Warheads', paper presented to the conference 'Reykjavik Revisited: Steps Toward a World Free of Nuclear Weapons', Hoover Institution, Stanford University, CA, 24–25 October 2007; Raymond Juzaitis and John McLaughlin, 'Challenges of Verification and Compliance within a State of Universal Latency', paper presented to the conference 'Reykjavik Revisited: Steps Toward a World Free of Nuclear Weapons'; Patricia M. Lewis, 'Verification of Nuclear Weapon Elimination', in Karp (ed.), *Security Without Nuclear Weapons? Different Perspectives on Non-Nuclear Security*; Tom Milne and Henrietta Wilson, 'Verifying the Transition from Low Levels of Nuclear Weapons to a Nuclear Weapon-Free World', VERTIC Research Report no. 2, June 1999; Theodore Taylor, 'Technological Problems of Verification', in Steinberger, Udgaonkar and Rotblat (eds), *A Nuclear-Weapon-Free World: Desirable? Feasible?*; Taylor, 'Verified Elimination of Nuclear Warheads', *Science and Global Security*, vol. 1, nos. 1–2, 1989, pp. 1–26, http://www.princeton.edu/~globsec/ publications/pdf/1_1-2Taylor.pdf; and Zarimpas (ed.), *Transparency in Nuclear Warheads and Materials*, Part II.

13   Fetter, 'Stockpile Declarations', in Zarimpas (ed.), *Transparency in Nuclear Warheads and Materials*.

14   Eric R. Gerdes, Roger G. Johnston and James E. Doyle, 'A Proposed Approach for Monitoring Nuclear Warhead Dismantlement', *Science and Global Security*, vol. 9, no. 2, 2001, pp. 113–41, http://www.princeton.edu/~globsec/ publications/pdf/9_2gerdes.pdf.

15   John R. Walker, 'Chemical Weapons Verification: The UK's Practice Challenge Inspection Programme at Government Facilities', in J.B. Poole (ed.), *Verification Report 1991: Yearbook on Arms Control and Environmental Agreements* (Tallahassee, FL: Apex Press for VERTIC, 1991).

16   Oleg Bukharin, 'The Changing Russian and US Nuclear Weapon Complexes: Challenges for Transparency', in Zarimpas (ed.), *Transparency in Nuclear Warheads and Materials*, pp. 189–96.

17   Juzaitis and McLaughlin, 'Challenges of Verification and Compliance within a State of Universal Latency'.

18   Johnston, 'Tamper-Indicating Seals for Nuclear Disarmament and Hazardous Waste Management', *Science and Global Security*, vol. 9, no. 2, 2001, pp. 93–112, http://www.princeton.edu/~globsec/ publications/pdf/9_2johnston.pdf. It is also worth noting that physical containment does not allow a state to *prove* that it has not diverted nuclear material in the same way that material accountancy can. But in large facilities, such as Japan's Rokkasho reprocessing plant, which handles so much plutonium

that, given the measurement errors that exist, material accountancy is unable to effectively keep track of it all, the primary safeguard is containment, a much-criticised arrangement.

19 Office of Nonproliferation Research and Engineering, 'Technology R&D for Arms Control', *Arms Control and Nonproliferation Technologies*, Spring 2001, pp. 4–17, http://www.fas.org/sgp/othergov/doe/acnt/2001.pdf; Committee on International Security and Arms Control, *Monitoring Nuclear Weapons and Nuclear Explosive Materials: An Assessment of Methods and Capabilities*, pp. 97–108.

20 The Nuclear Material Identification System developed at the US Oak Ridge National Laboratory is capable of measuring masses and so could, in theory, be used by international inspectors if nuclear-armed states declassified the quantity of fissile material in their warheads. However, the ability to measure masses comes at the expense of a considerable increase in complexity. Such an increase is undesirable in an international verification context, as it makes it much more difficult for inspectors to ensure that the verification system is operating as designed and has not been rigged as part of an effort to violate an agreement. See Office of Nonproliferation Research and Engineering, 'Technology R&D for Arms Control', p. 7. Robust containment measures certainly reduce fears that a state could remove fissile material from a warhead after it has entered the verification system. A state could, however, always divert fissile material before such containment measures had been put in place.

21 For a good discussion of the attribute v. template debate, see Bukharin, 'Russian and US Technology Development in Support of Nuclear Warhead and Material Transparency Initiatives', in Zarimpas (ed.), *Transparency in Nuclear Warheads and Materials*, pp. 166–73.

22 In July 1989, the Soviet Union found it in its interests to permit measurement of a nuclear warhead without information barriers. See Steve Fetter, Thomas B. Cochran, Lee Grodzins, Harvey L. Lynch and Martin S. Zucker, 'Gamma-Ray Measurements of a Soviet Cruise-Missile Warhead', *Science*, vol. 248, no. 4,957, 18 May 1990, pp. 828–34.

23 'Verification of Nuclear Disarmament: Final Report on Studies into the Verification of Nuclear Warheads and their Components', working paper submitted by the UK to the 2005 Review Conference of the Parties to the Treaty on the Non-Proliferation of Nuclear Weapons, NPT/CONF.2005/WP.1, 18 April 2005, http://www.reachingcriticalwill.org/legal/npt/RevCon05/wp/verification_UK.pdf; Bukharin and Doyle, 'Verification of the Shutdown or Converted Status of Excess Warhead Production Capacity: Technology Options and Policy Issues', *Science and Global Security*, vol. 10, no. 2, 2002, pp. 103–24, http://www.princeton.edu/~globsec/publications/pdf/10_2%20103%20124%20bUKHARIN.pdf.

24 Under the INF treaty, for instance, US and Russian inspectors verified the destruction of delivery systems, ensured that missile-production facilities were not being used to produce prohibited delivery vehicles and inspected military bases for nuclear materials.

25 Bukharin and Doyle, 'Transparency and Predictability Measures for US and Russian Strategic Arms Reductions', *The Nonproliferation Review*, vol. 9, no. 2, Summer 2002, pp. 82–100, http://cns.miis.edu/pubs/npr/vol09/92/92bukh.pdf.

26 The possibility of declared facilities being used for proscribed purposes was recognised at least as early as 1959, during early UK discussions of the feasibility of disarmament. Private communication, UK government official, April 2008.

27 Thomas W. Wood, Bruce D. Reid, John L. Smoot and James L. Fuller, 'Establishing Confident Accounting for Russian Weapons Plutonium', *The Nonproliferation Review*, vol. 9, no. 2, Summer 2002,

p. 134, http://cns.miis.edu/pubs/npr/vol09/92/92wood.pdf.

28 Ibid., pp. 128–33; Fetter, 'Nuclear Archaeology: Verifying Declarations of Fissile-Material Production', Science and Global Security, vol. 3, nos. 3–4, 1993, pp. 240–4, http://www.princeton.edu/~globsec/publications/pdf/3_3-4Fetter.pdf.

29 For an example of how this issue is presented to media, see the attempts by British Nuclear Fuels to explain why material had 'gone missing' from the Sellafield nuclear site in Cumbria. British Nuclear Fuels PLC, 'Media Response: Publication of Materials Unaccounted For', 13 August 2005, http://www.bnfl.com/content.php?pageID=49&newsID=70.

30 The US gives figures for the mass of the isotope U-235. The UK figures relate to the total quantity of HEU.

31 US Department of Energy, 'Plutonium: The First 50 Years: United States Plutonium Production, Acquisition, and Utilization from 1944 through 1994', DOE/DP-0137, February 1996, http://www.fissilematerials.org/ipfm/site_down/doe96.pdf; US Department of Energy, 'Highly Enriched Uranium: Striking a Balance: A Historical Report on the United States Highly Enriched Uranium Production, Acquisition, and Utilization Activities from 1945 through September 30, 1996', draft, revision 1, January 2001, http://www.fissilematerials.org/ipfm/site_down/doe01.pdf; UK Ministry of Defence, 'Historical Accounting for UK Defence Highly Enriched Uranium', March 2006, http://www.fissilematerials.org/ipfm/site_down/mod06.pdf; UK Ministry of Defence, 'Plutonium and Aldermaston: An Historical Account', 2000, http://www.fas.org/news/uk/000414-uk2.htm.

32 Experience from Project Sapphire (a US programme to recover HEU from Kazakhstan) suggests that uncertainties in the Russian fissile-material stock might be around 4% – enough for around 4,000 warheads. See Michael Brown, 'Phased Nuclear Disarmament and US Defense Policy', Henry L. Stimson Center, Occasional Paper no. 30, October 1996, p. 17, http://www.stimson.org/wmd/pdf/brown.pdf.

33 Private communication, 16 April 2008.

34 The declarations do not give the quantity of HEU used in detonations, so the figures for HEU are based on the assumption that three times more HEU than plutonium was consumed.

35 Robert J. Einhorn, 'Controlling Fissile Materials and Ending Nuclear Testing', paper presented to the conference, 'Achieving the Vision of a World Free of Nuclear Weapons: International Conference on Nuclear Disarmament', Oslo, 26–27 March 2008, http://disarmament.nrpa.no/wp-content/uploads/2008/02/Paper_Einhorn.pdf.

36 CWC, Verification Annex, Part X, para. 41.

37 John Carlson and Russell Leslie, 'Special Inspections Revisited', paper presented to the Institute of Nuclear Materials Management 2005 symposium, Phoenix, AZ, July 2005, http://www.asno.dfat.gov.au/publications/inmm2005_special_inspections.pdf. Partly in recognition of these problems associated with special inspections, 'complementary access', a provision of the Additional Protocol (see note 41 below), was, to some extent, designed as an alternative. However, there are important limitations to the verification techniques that inspectors can employ during a complementary-access visit and, significantly, states are allowed to refuse access and satisfy inspectors instead 'through alternative means' – whether appropriate such means will always exist is very doubtful. See IAEA, 'Model Protocol Additional to the Agreement(s) between States and the International Atomic Energy Agency for the Application of Safeguards', INFCIRC/540 (Corrected), September 1997, Article 5(c), http://www.iaea.org/Publications/Documents/Infcircs/1997/infcirc540c.pdf.

38 Richard L. Garwin, 'Technologies and Procedures for Verifying Warhead Status and Dismantlement', in Zarimpas (ed.), *Transparency in Nuclear Warheads and Materials*, p. 152.

39 Jeffrey T. Richelson, *Spying on the Bomb* (New York: W. W. Norton & Company, 2007), pp. 521–4.

40 Wyn Q. Bowen, *Libya and Nuclear Proliferation: Stepping back from the brink*, Adelphi Paper 380 (Abingdon: Routledge for the IISS, 2006), pp. 65–6.

41 The Additional Protocol is a further (currently optional) agreement for NPT signatories, designed to give the IAEA the tools it needs to be able to draw credible conclusions about whether a state is conducting clandestine nuclear activities. As of 30 May 2008, 88 states had an Additional Protocol in force.

42 Quoted in Darryl Howlett and John Simpson, 'Nuclearisation and Denuclearisation in South Africa', *Survival*, vol. 35, no. 3, Autumn 1993, p. 167.

43 IAEA, 'The Agency's Verification Activities in South Africa', GOV/2684, 8 September 1993, para. 29.

44 Adolf von Baeckmann, Gary Dillon and Demetrius Perricos, 'Nuclear Verification in South Africa', *IAEA Bulletin*, vol. 37, no. 1, 1995, http://www.iaea.org/Publications/Magazines/Bulletin/Bull371/37105394248.pdf; Howlett and Simpson, 'Nuclearisation and Denuclearisation in South Africa'.

45 Private communications with current and former UK and US officials, London, November 2007.

46 These would be broader than the fissile-material and warhead declarations discussed above in that they would be expected to tell the story of the entire programme in all its aspects, not just declare current stocks and past fissile-material production and use.

47 Private communication with a UK official, London, November 2007.

48 Though states are as a result under no explicit obligation to make nuclear personnel available for interview under the CTBT, a state could do so as a way of demonstrating its willingness to meet its Article IV.57 obligation 'to make every reasonable effort to demonstrate its compliance with [the] Treaty'.

49 In particular, Iran refused to grant an interview with one of the former heads of its Physics Research Centre.

50 See for example Rotblat, 'Societal Verification', in Steinberger, Udgaonkar and Rotblat (eds), *A Nuclear-Weapon-Free World: Desirable? Feasible?*.

51 Private communication with Doyle, London, November 2007.

52 Private communication with Fetter, London, November 2007.

53 Private communication with UK official, London, November 2007.

54 It is difficult to find a more exact estimate, but $1 billion appears to be the right order of magnitude, given that the verification system has been under construction since 1996, the bulk of it is now complete, and the annual budget for the Preparatory Commission for the Comprehensive Nuclear-Test-Ban Treaty Organization is currently around $100 million (the majority of which is spent on developing the verification system).

55 Tariq Rauf, 'A Cut-Off of Production of Weapons-Usable Fissionable Material: Considerations, Requirements and IAEA Capabilities', statement to the Conference on Disarmament, Geneva, 24 August 2006, p. 26, http://www.reachingcriticalwill.org/political/cd/speeches06/24AugustIAEA.pdf.

56 Steven M. Kosiak, *Spending on US Strategic Nuclear Forces: Plans & Options for the 21st Century* (Washington DC: Center for Strategic and Budgetary Assessments, 2006), p. i, http://www.csbaonline.org/4Publications/PubLibrary/R.20060901.Spending_on_US_Str/R.20060901.Spending_on_US_Str.pdf.

57 The $3.5bn figure only includes the cost of 'directed stockpile work' and six supporting 'campaigns' (which encompass various weapons-related

activities) and excludes the cost of support facilities such as the Dual-Axis Radiographic Hydrodynamic Test Facility. US Department of Energy/National Nuclear Security Administration, 'FY 2008 Congressional Budget Request', Volume 1, DOE-CF014, February 2007, p. 59, http://www.cfo.doe. gov/budget/08budget/Content/Volumes/ Vol_1_NNSA.pdf.

Chapter Three

1   One exception was the McCloy–Zorin Accords, signed in September 1961 by the US and the Soviet Union, which set out a series of 'principles as the basis for future multilateral negotiations on disarmament'. For a summary of the various abolitionist movements that there have been over the decades, see Michael Krepon, 'Ban the Bomb. Really.', *The American Interest*, vol. 3, no. 3, January–February 2008, pp. 88–93.

2   James M. Acton, 'Strengthening Safeguards and Nuclear Disarmament: Is There a Connection?', *The Nonproliferation Review*, vol. 14, no. 3, November 2007, pp. 525–35.

3   See for example UN Secretary-General Kofi Annan, 'Address to the Nuclear Non-Proliferation Treaty Review Conference', New York, 2 May 2005, http://www. un.org/events/npt2005/statements/ npt02sg.

4   · The World Nuclear Association represents and promotes the nuclear industry and the Nuclear Threat Initiative is an NGO working on reducing the risk of use and preventing the proliferation of nuclear, biological and chemical weapons. It is co-chaired by former US Senator Sam Nunn and Cable News Network founder Ted Turner.

5   Tariq Rauf and Zoryana Vovchok, 'Fuel for Thought', *IAEA Bulletin*, vol. 49, no. 2, March 2008, pp. 33–7, to appear at http:// www.iaea.org/Publications/Magazines/ Bulletin/.

6   Mark Hibbs and Ann MacLachlan, 'Vendors' Relative Risk Rising in New Nuclear Power Markets', *Nucleonics Week*, vol. 48, no. 3, 18 January 2007. See also Sharon Squassoni, 'The Realities of Nuclear Expansion', Testimony before the US House of Representatives Select Committee on Energy Independence and Global Warming, 12 March 2008, pp. 7–10, http://www.carnegieendowment. org/files/3-12-08_squassoni_testimony1. pdf.

7   Iran's centrifuge programme was initiated in 1985 and was still fairly embryonic when it was revealed in 2002. IAEA, 'Implementation of the NPT Safeguards Agreement in the Islamic Republic of Iran: Report by the Director General', GOV/2004/83, 15 November 2004, para. 23, http://www.iaea.org/Publications/ Documents/Board/2004/gov2004-83. pdf. Although there may be a number of reasons for this slow pace of development, one must surely be the inherent difficulty of centrifuge technology. For a discussion of Libya's centrifuge programme, see Bowen, '*Libya and Nuclear Proliferation: Stepping back from the brink*', Chapter 2.

8   Mahdi Obeidi and Kurt Pitzer, *The Bomb in My Garden* (Hoboken, NJ: John Wiley & Sons, 2004), Chapters 3–6.

9   See Jack Boureston and Charles D. Ferguson, 'Separation Anxiety (Laser Enrichment)', *Bulletin of the Atomic Scientists*, vol. 61, no. 2, March–April 2005, pp. 14–18, http://thebulletin.metapress. com/content/p3v65u514051j882/fulltext. pdf (since this article was published, General Electric has acquired the rights to the SILEX laser-enrichment process). See also Allan S. Krass, Peter Boskma, Boelie Elzen and Wim A. Smit,

Uranium Enrichment and Nuclear Weapon Proliferation (London: Taylor and Francis for SIPRI, 1983), Chapter 2, http://www.sipri.org/contents/publications/Krass83/Krass83.pdf.

[10] See for example 'Nuclear Safeguards: In Pursuit of the Undoable', *Economist* (US edition), vol. 384, no. 8,543, 25 August 2007, p. 56. For a critique of the current state of nuclear safeguards, see Henry Sokolski (ed.), *Falling Behind: International Scrutiny of the Peaceful Atom* (Carlisle, PA: Strategic Studies Institute, February 2008), http://www.npec-web.org/Books/20080327-FallingBehind.pdf.

[11] James Acton and Joanna Little, 'The Use of Voluntary Safeguards to Build Trust in States' Nuclear Programmes: The Case of Iran', *Verification Matters*, no. 8, May 2007, pp. 31–2, http://www.vertic.org/publications/VM8.pdf.

[12] Jill N. Cooley, 'Integrated Nuclear Safeguards: Genesis and Evolution', in Trevor Findlay (ed.), *Verification Yearbook 2003* (London: VERTIC, 2003) pp. 38–9, http://www.vertic.org/assets/YB03/VY03_Cooley.pdf.

[13] In states with an Additional Protocol in force, this target is relaxed once the IAEA has concluded that there are no undeclared nuclear materials in the state. See *ibid*.

[14] The worst-case scenario would involve a state doing each of the following before it diverted nuclear material: (i) fully designing a nuclear weapon; (ii) manufacturing all the non-nuclear components for the weapon; and (iii) mastering the technology for fabricating the nuclear-weapon pit. In such a scenario, the time between diverting the material and manufacturing the nuclear weapon might be days or even hours. China, for instance, manufactured its first pit in one day. Even if air strikes could be organised in this short time, they could only be effective if the location of the weapons facility was known (a questionable prospect).

[15] James Acton and Carter Newman, 'IAEA Verification of Military Research and Development', *Verification Matters*, no. 5, July 2006, http://www.vertic.org/publications/VM5%20(2).pdf.

[16] For instance, Marvin Miller and Jack Ruina have written that 'The only real control of breakout in a [nuclear-weapons-free world] is strict international control of all facilities for the production of fissionable materials that could be used in nuclear weapons.' Marvin Miller and Jack Ruina, 'The Breakout Problem', in Steinberger, Udgaonkar and Rotblat (eds), *A Nuclear-Weapon-Free World: Desirable? Feasible?*, p. 101.

[17] For an example of some preliminary discussions, see IAEA, 'Multilateral Approaches to the Nuclear Fuel Cycle: Expert Group Report submitted to the Director General of the International Atomic Energy Agency', INFCIRC/640, 22 February 2005, http://www.iaea.org/Publications/Documents/Infcircs/2005/infcirc640.pdf.

[18] Walker, 'Destination Unknown: Rokkasho and the International Future of Nuclear Reprocessing', *International Affairs*, vol. 82, no. 4, July 2006, pp. 743–61.

[19] Frans Berkhout and William Walker, 'Safeguards at Nuclear Bulk Handling Facilities', in J.B. Poole and R. Guthrie (eds), *Verification Report 1992: Yearbook on Arms Control and Environmental Agreements* (London: VERTIC, 1992). Reprocessing technologies that do not produce separated plutonium (such as the UREX+ process) are currently under development. How proliferation-resistant these technologies are is, however, a controversial issue. See for instance Frank von Hippel, 'Managing Spent Fuel in the United States: The Illogic of Reprocessing', International Panel on Fissile Materials, Research Report no. 3, January 2007, pp. 20–4, http://www.fissilematerials.org/ipfm/site_down/ipfmresearchreport03.pdf.

[20] Matthew Bunn, John P. Holdren, Steve Fetter and Bob van der Zwaan, 'The Economics of Reprocessing versus Direct Disposal of Spent Nuclear Fuel', *Nuclear Technology*, vol. 150, no. 3, June 2005,

pp. 209–30, http://www.puaf.umd.edu/
Fetter/2005-NT-repro.pdf.

21 See *ibid* for a contrary view. These
authors argue that reprocessing will
remain uneconomic, because the cost
of extracting uranium from seawater –
which, they judge, would remain a viable
option when other uranium sources
were depleted – is lower than the cost of
reprocessing.

22 Bunn, *Securing the Bomb 2007* (Cambridge,
MA and Washington DC: Project on

Managing the Atom, Harvard University
and Nuclear Threat Initiative, September
2007), pp. 37–9 and 72–7, http://www.nti.
org/e_research/securingthebomb07.pdf;
von Hippel, 'A Comprehensive Approach
to Elimination of Highly-Enriched-
Uranium from All Nuclear-Reactor Fuel
Cycles', *Science and Global Security*, vol.
12, no. 3, 2004, pp. 137–64, http://www.
princeton.edu/~globsec/publications/
pdf/12-3_von%20Hippel_SGS_137-164.
pdf.

Chapter Four

1 Report of the Canberra Commission on
the Elimination of Nuclear Weapons
(Canberra: Commonwealth of Australia,
August 1996), p. 63, http://www.dfat.gov.
au/cc/CCREPORT.PDF.

2 *Securing Our Survival: The Case for a
Nuclear Weapons Convention*, pp. 109–17.

3 *Ibid.*, p. 110.

4 List adapted from Bruce D. Larkin,
*Designing Denuclearization: An Interpretive
Encyclopedia* (New Brunswick, NJ:
Transaction, 2008), p. 99.

5 US General Kevin Chilton's remark that
the US needs to retain nuclear weapons
as long as anyone has enough nuclear
weapons to destroy the US 'way of life'
implicitly recognises this possibility.
See Chapter 1, pp. 16–17 and 'US Needs
Nuclear Weapons for Rest of Century:
General'.

6 Though the Bush administration argued
that that the deal was, in fact, good
for non-proliferation, partly because it
brought India into the non-proliferation
mainstream.

7 For a more detailed review of NPT
withdrawal issues, see George Bunn and
John B. Rhinelander, 'NPT Withdrawal:
Time for the Security Council to Step
In', *Arms Control Today*, vol. 35, no. 4,
May 2005, http://www.armscontrol.org/
act/2005_05/Bunn_Rhinelander.asp.

8 Many such proposals have been
submitted as working papers to NPT
review and preparatory conferences,
and are available on the website of the
Reaching Critical Will project, http://
www.reachingcriticalwill.org/legal/
npt/nptindex1.html. See in particular
'Strengthening the NPT Against
Withdrawal and Non-Compliance:
Suggestions for the Establishment of
Procedures and Mechanisms', working
paper submitted by Germany to the
Preparatory Committee for the 2005
Review Conference of the Parties to
the Treaty on the Non-Proliferation of
Nuclear Weapons, NPT/CONF.2005/
PC.III/WP.15, 29 April 2004, http://
www.reachingcriticalwill.org/legal/npt/
prepcom04/papers/GermanyWP15.pdf.

9 Einhorn, paper presented to the conference
'The Crisis in Nonproliferation: Meeting
the Challenge'. For an account of the
history of this proposal, see Bunn and
Rhinelander, 'NPT Withdrawal: Time for
the Security Council to Step In'.

10 Pierre Goldschmidt, 'The Urgent
Need to Strengthen the Nuclear Non-
Proliferation Regime', *Policy Outlook*
no. 25, Carnegie Endowment for
International Peace, January 2006, http://
www.carnegieendowment.org/files/
PO25.Goldschmidt.FINAL2.pdf.

11 George Shultz, concluding remarks to the conference 'Achieving the Vision of a World Free of Nuclear Weapons: International Conference on Nuclear Disarmament', Oslo, Norway, 26–27 February 2008.

Chapter Five

1 For a discussion of the non-democratic pattern of nuclear rollback, see the concluding chapter of Perkovich, *India's Nuclear Bomb* (Berkeley, CA: University of California Press, 2001 edition).

2 Roger D. Speed, *The International Control of Nuclear Weapons* (Stanford: Center for International Security and Arms Control, June 1994).

3 Jonathan Schell, 'The Abolition', in Schell, *The Fate of the Earth and the Abolition* (Stanford, CA: Stanford University Press, 2000). See also Michael J. Mazarr, 'Virtual Nuclear Arsenals', *Survival*, vol. 37, no. 3, Autumn 1995, pp. 7–26.

4 Christopher A. Ford, 'Disarmament and Non-Nuclear Stability in Tomorrow's World', remarks to a conference on disarmament and non-proliferation issues, Nagasaki, Japan, 31 August 2007, www.state.gov/t/isn/rls/rm/92733.htm.

5 Donald MacKenzie and Graham Spinardi, 'Tacit Knowledge, Weapons Design and the Uninvention of Nuclear Weapons', *American Journal of Sociology*, vol. 101, no. 1, July 2005, pp. 44–99. A useful parallel might be drawn (courtesy of Dr John Walker of the UK Foreign and Commonwealth Office) with experimental archaeology, in which it is sometimes necessary to essentially reinvent certain aspects of ancient or medieval building techniques, because their 'secrets' have been forgotten.

Conclusions

1 Brown, 'New Nuclear Realities', pp. 15–17.

2 See in this regard the pointed remark of North Korean leader Kim Il Sung that 'all US military activities are nuclear in nature because they are backed by nuclear weapons'. Katy Oh, presentation to the Institute for Defense Analysis, 25 March 2008.

⌒IISS ADELPHI PAPERS

RECENT **ADELPHI PAPERS** INCLUDE:

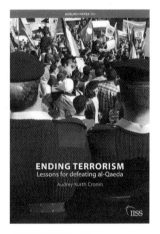

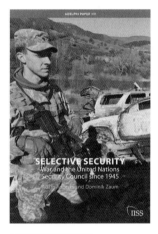

The Evolution of Strategic Thought
Classic Adelphi Papers

The Adelphi Papers monograph series is the Institute's principal contribution to policy-relevant, original academic research. Collected on the occasion of the Institute's 50th anniversary, the twelve Adelphi Papers in this volume represent some of the finest examples of writing on strategic issues. They offer insights into the changing security landscape of the past half-century and glimpses of some of the most significant security events and trends of our times, from the Cold War nuclear arms race, through the oil crisis of 1973, to the contemporary challenge of asymmetric war in Iraq and Afghanistan.

Published April 2008; 704 pp.

Bookpoint Ltd. 130 Milton Park, Abingdon, Oxon OX14 4SB, UK
Tel: +44 (0)1235 400524, Fax: +44 (0)1235 400525
Customer orders: book.orders@tandf.co.uk
Bookshops, wholesalers and agents:
Email (UK): uktrade@tandf.co.uk,
email (international): international@tandf.co.uk

Routledge
Taylor & Francis Group

IISS   THE INTERNATIONAL INSTITUTE FOR STRATEGIC STUDIES